PRETTY YOUNG

PRETTY YOUNG

BEING UNAPOLOGETICALLY
FEMALE IN A MAN'S WORLD

SARAH WHITNEY HUMPHREY

NEW DEGREE PRESS

COPYRIGHT © 2021 SARAH WHITNEY HUMPHREY
All rights reserved.

PRETTY YOUNG
Being Unapologetically Female in a Man's World

ISBN	978-1-63730-435-8	Paperback
	978-1-63730-527-0	Kindle Ebook
	978-1-63730-528-7	Ebook

To my future daughter(s)—this one is for you. <3

TABLE OF CONTENTS

―

INTRODUCTION 9

CHAPTER 1.   FACT OR FEELING? 19
CHAPTER 2.   CULTURAL PRESSURES 33
CHAPTER 3.   YOUR LIMITING BELIEFS ARE LIMITING
             YOU IN MORE WAYS THAN ONE 43
CHAPTER 4.   REDEFINING BEAUTY ON
             YOUR OWN TERMS 53
CHAPTER 5.   THE TOXIC TANGO 63
CHAPTER 6.   #METOO 73
CHAPTER 7.   SEXY & I OWN IT! 85
CHAPTER 8.   FAITH, SHAME & THE PATRIARCHY 97
CHAPTER 9.   THE MENTAL HEALTH PANDEMIC 111
CHAPTER 10. POST-GRAD & A PANDEMIC 119
CHAPTER 11. ALONE OR LONELY? 129
CHAPTER 12. VALIDATION IS FOR PARKING 139
CHAPTER 13. WOMEN IN THE WORKPLACE: LACK OF
             CONFIDENCE & GENDER BIASES 151
CHAPTER 14. WOMEN IN THE WORKPLACE: A NEW
             ERA OF ENTREPRE-ISTAS 161

CONCLUSION 173
ACKNOWLEDGMENTS 177
APPENDIX 179

INTRODUCTION

―

My best friend, Natalie, started a drinking game in my honor. It's called *take a shot every time someone tells Sarah he's seen her at the gym*. Needless to say, you might be blacked out by the end of the night.

During college, almost every guy I ever met started off with, "I think I've seen you in the gym before." Now, I'm not sure why they couldn't come up with a better pickup line, but regardless, I was apparently *that* girl. I was that short, blonde girl from the gym who could be categorized as "hot" or "attractive" by society's standards.

During my first two and a half years of college, this attention I was getting honestly amazed me. In middle school and high school, I was very much the girl who flew underneath the radar. I was never popular. I wasn't the skinniest. I was never at all the parties. I barely even drank. I felt invisible to the outside world. When I went to college, I was desperate for things to change. I wanted to be seen and to be known. I wanted to be wanted. So, on a mission to make it happen, I did all the things you are "supposed" to do. I joined a sorority, went to parties, got drunk, and hooked up with boys. For a while, I was having the time of my life. This newfound attention was like having alcohol for the first time: intoxicating and liberating.

Unfortunately, this attention also went to my head. My ego was at an all-time high, even though I would never admit that to anyone. I was doing the best I could to live up to the labels given to me, and honestly, I was succeeding. I played my part so well I could've beat out Emma Stone for an Oscar. I put a smile on my face when I needed to. I was friendly and bubbly. I was fashion-forward and always looked put together. I did well in my classes and received high marks from my teachers. I was "perfect," or so it seemed.

That all came crashing down on me during the second semester of my sophomore year. Heartbreak and trauma soon became my reality, and I was holding my exterior self together by a thread. My crippling anxiety and depression I had dealt with for so long in high school began to overtake my everyday life. The eating disorder I thought I had recovered from began to creep back in.

Maybe if I lost some more weight, no one would know I'm actually hurting? I thought. *Maybe that guy who broke my heart would actually love me if I was skinnier?*

I began to party more because drowning out our worries is what we are supposed to do, right? I spent hours scrolling through social media, comparing my short, athletic build to those with taller, leaner figures. I continually let boys disrespect me because nice girls are supposed to shut their mouths and take it, right? My anxiety and depression got worse with each passing day. Even sitting in class would make my heart race at a thousand miles per hour. To top it all off, I got a concussion I deliberately ignored. My mental, emotional, and physical health were deteriorating. Somehow, despite all the hurt and pain, I tried my best to maintain that perfect facade even though I was falling apart at the seams.

Each day, as I passed by familiar and friendly faces, I'd greet everyone happily with a big smile because that is what I thought I was supposed to do, despite feeling more alone, more broken, and more shattered every day. I soon felt suffocated by both myself and others as these different labels were continuously imposed on me—the "pretty" girl, the "smart" girl, the "bubbly" girl. People had told me for so long that I must be all those things. When I felt like I no longer fit the mold, I felt like a failure.

I spent so much of my life trying to live up to a standard and fit into labels others placed on me. While certain standards and labels can be debilitating for people like myself, I can understand why people like labels.

It's safe. It creates a sense of order. It makes life easier to understand, but for me, labels feel suffocating.

Who do they want me to be? Who should I be? These thoughts pounded in my head constantly.

But in actuality, the real question should have been: *Who do I want to be?*

For people of all generations, it can be difficult to know who we are and who we want to be. But for young millennials and Gen Z'ers alike, this difficulty is apparent now more than ever. Our generation not only has parents, friends, cultural pressures, societal norms, and religion cramming ideologies down our throats, but also has social media, which is its own beast. I, like so many others, have spent so much time deliberating exactly who I am, who I want to be, who I should be, and where I'm going. I'm a professional overthinker and, to my own dismay, have seemingly taken every opinion into consideration at least once.

While it is easy for me to dread the fact that I do this, I only exhibit behaviors I have been conditioned to believe are acceptable, from seeking validation to accepting these socially and culturally constructed labels. We have been fed false narratives. Whether the narrative is about looking a certain way or pressuring people to have jobs before graduating college, these narratives are fed to us by people who we think we can trust, such as our teachers, parents, government officials, priests, rabbis, you name it. For women especially, these narratives create most of the mental noise and distractions swirling around in our heads.

One major issue with young women is we go through life on autopilot, never questioning, pondering, or seeking more information. Rather, we accept what is. We accept these boundaries, wear the labels, and find contentment in the ordinary. We stay in our boxes and rarely cross the line into unknown territory. We overthink but rarely become introspective because knowing ourselves can be the most terrifying thing of all. We are taught to sit there and look pretty. We are taught to wait for that dream guy, dream job, or dream house.

"Don't be bossy," they say, "or you might come across as bitchy."
"Don't be too smart, or you might intimidate the man."
"Don't excel in your career so much, or you won't be able to take proper care of your children."
"You can't have it all."

Rather than fight these voices speaking lies in our heads, we stay silent and mind our own business. But what if we started asking the questions, like: *Why do I keep going from one toxic relationship to the other? Why am I constantly falling into these negative ongoing cycles? Do I really believe everything my religious or spiritual practice has to say about God or a higher power? Why do I feel the need to prove myself and find validation from everyone around me? Who was I before the world told me to be something else?* The list goes on and on.

We live in an era where we are bombarded with so many distractions and noise. From scrolling through social media, to seeing various national events unfold, to trying to meet our family's expectations, to keeping up with our own personal life and obligations, our world seems to be wildly spinning at times, affecting our emotional, mental, physical, and spiritual health.

This is what your twenties are like, they say. It's full of chaos and confusion, frustration and liberation. It's known to be the era of both being a hot mess and settling down. Both descriptions are contradictions of each other, yet they are far too accurate. We party to forget and get married because we think we have to. We work a nine-to-five job to pay the bills, but we drown out the mundanity of the life we signed up for with booze and boys.

The mental noise and distractions women experience eat away at us, yet we are so unaware. We rarely take the time to stop, reflect, and question our thoughts and behaviors. We have become so accustomed to how things are that many of us have stopped questioning why it has to be this way, why we often belittle ourselves, and why we can't find the confidence within ourselves to take the leap.

We feed into the preconceived notions of what it means to be a woman and no longer have our own opinions on the matter, yet we still wonder why we struggle deep down. We still wonder why we don't feel completely fulfilled. We still wonder, what if? What if we did it a different way? What if we went against the norm? But "what if" is often too much of a scary idea to act on. So, we stay in these toxic cycles, we continue down the path set before us, and we sit there and look pretty.

Because we've become accustomed to the noise and distractions, women have to drown out their truest selves. I am a firm believer in this being why so many women struggle with body image and mental health and toxic relationships. We have found our worth in what others say rather than who we truly are.

For the longest time, I felt alone when it came to how I thought about life. I felt like I was the only one who struggled with self-worth and self-confidence. I thought I was the only one who wanted a life outside of the norm. But according to some troubling statistics, I discovered I was never alone. According to a study done by Dove, only "4 percent of women worldwide consider themselves 'beautiful.' By the age of 17, 78 percent of teens have a negative view of their bodies." In another related study, researchers found when women enter the workplace, their confidence actually decreases over time, from 27 percent as a new employee to a mere 13 percent as a more seasoned employee. When it comes to getting a promotion, men are more likely to apply when they feel 60 percent confident they will get the position, whereas women tend to apply only when they feel 100 percent confident they will get the position (Slaughter, 2016).

Why is it as women we have such negative views of ourselves? Why do we diminish our abilities, when in actuality we are more than capable? Why do we believe we cannot succeed when we can? Why do we believe in these false narratives and give into our own mental noise and distractions, rather than work hard to disrupt the noise and counter these socially-constructed diversions?

We live in a society that is so fast paced, but we ignore the red flags, put our blinders on, and carry on with our lives. Our pain manifests as eating disorders, mental illness, toxic relationships, or poor self-esteem. We are left crying out for help. With these neglected personal issues, a global pandemic, and a stark political and civil divide in our nation, we have what I believe is the biggest threat to our generation's mental, emotional, physical, and spiritual health to date.

So many of us are carrying around baggage from our own brokenness and the brokenness of others, which only inhibits us from achieving all we can be. The saying goes, "Hurt people hurt people." With the vast amount of hurt and pain women experience every day, it can be easy for us to project our hurt and our pain on others unintentionally. Our hurt ends up hurting the ones we love the most.

But that's when you have to stop yourself and ask: What if? What if women took the time to pause for just a moment, long enough to take inventory of their life? What if women took the time to declutter their minds and decipher their own thoughts? What if women spent the time to do internal work and question life as they know it, rather than repress every emotion and feeling that comes their way? What if women could bring light to the false narratives and silence the mental noise and distractions perpetuated by sexist ideologies, men, parents, or society? What if women could walk into a version of their truest self, confidently and unapologetically? What if?

My main goal throughout this book is to dive into the not-so-pretty struggles and mental noise and distractions young women face. After graduating college, I had a little stint in the corporate world and would constantly hear people advising others to keep professional and personal life separate. While I think that is true to an extent, your overall well-being will undoubtedly overflow into every aspect of your life to varying degrees. Your mental, emotional, physical, and spiritual health are all intertwined, and when one is off-kilter, everything is out of balance.

As a twenty-three-year-old writing this, I surely do not claim to know all about life. I cry often. I have daily existential crises. I lie in bed some nights hoping my life will matter. But that is also why I'm the best person to be writing this book. I'm in the thick of it all. I know what it's like to pick yourself up time and time again, even when it feels like doing so might actually break your heart into a million pieces. I know what it's like to feel like everyone around you doesn't get it. I know what it feels like to want love and acceptance so badly you'll do just about anything to get it. I know how it feels to be so passionate about your own desires and dreams, only to have them questioned by the people who love you the most.

Growing up is hard, but I've learned the growing never stops, which is a tremendously beautiful thing. Life allows you a million and ten chances, and it's up to us to go out and grab them. The only way you'll take full advantage of those chances is by fully uncovering and addressing your struggles and the madness swirling around inside your mind. It's a lifelong process, really, and while it's never too late to start, it's easier if you start young.

By understanding where your own struggles and your own mental noise and distractions come from, you can begin to shape your reality into something more beautiful than you can even imagine. Women were made to be warriors, yet we are standing in our own way too often to see.

So, forget what they say. Forget—if only for a moment—we live in a society that says being pretty and young is glorious. Forget we live in a world where women are belittled for simply existing. Forget we live in a world where the pain and shame of your most personal experiences seem to define you. They don't. But for a moment, begin to ask yourself: Who? Who am I? Who was I before the world told me who to be?

I'm a firm believer that you know, deep down, you never had to be pretty. You never had to be young. You just had to be you.

CHAPTER ONE

FACT OR FEELING?

Have you ever wanted to be the "it girl"? For some people, it's always seemed like this far-off fantasy. It was someone you could pretend to be but never truly embody. It's one or the other. You're either in or you're out. You're the "it girl" or you're the "anti-it girl." So, at fifteen years old, Tavi Gevinson decided she would forever be the "anti-it girl."

Wearing heavy eyeliner and sporting blunt bangs, Tavi had angst written all over her. What better way to express these pent-up emotions than by creating an online publication for fellow angsty teens to find community in a world that simply did not understand them? With ambitions to deconstruct the patriarchy and revel in the rollercoaster that is teenage emotions, Tavi started *Style Rookie*, an online fashion publication.

Tavi noticed women of all ages are often misrepresented in the media through one-dimensional characters. Think of female archetypes like the perfect housewife trope or Superwoman. Both characters are perfect, yet often lack the relatability aspect of being human and flawed. Tavi stated, "One thing that can be very alienating about a misconception of feminism is that girls then think that to be a feminist, they have to live up to being perfectly consistent in your beliefs, never being insecure, never having doubts, having all of the answers" (Gevinson, 4:05).

In Tavi's eyes, *Style Rookie* was a discussion, not a rulebook. It was a place anyone could pitch their ideas, where girls could come to talk about fashion, culture, feminism, and the struggles of growing up in a world where society emphasizes beauty, wealth, and success. It was for the girls who didn't have it all figured out but wanted to learn.

Though Tavi considered *Style Rookie* to be a personal fashion blog, another large facet of the online publication was discovering what actually made a strong female character. Tavi often questioned how this idea of a strong female character often gets misinterpreted. Understanding that the media plays a huge role in shaping culture's definition of traditional societal structure—especially relating to the placement of women within that societal structure—Tavi published multiple blogs and advice columns, interviewed a diverse range of people, and created content that would push the cultural and societal boundaries of her millennial generation.

While giving a TED Talk, Tavi stated, "We get these two-dimensional superwomen who maybe have one quality that's played up a lot, like a Catwoman type. She plays her sexuality up a lot, and it's seen as power. But they're not strong characters who happen to be female. They're completely flat, and they're basically cardboard characters. The problem with this is that then people expect women to be that easy to understand, and women are mad at themselves for not being that simple, when, in actuality, women are complicated, women are multifaceted—not because women are crazy, but because people are crazy. And women happen to be people" (Gevinson, 1:10).

Women are not complicated; women are complex. We are not confusing; we are multifaceted. These words rang in my ears for hours on end. Hearing those words made it feel as if the dingy glass ceiling hovering above me—and all women—shattered into a million pieces. It was as if simply hearing those words began to deteriorate those fears and thoughts associated with my own identity. I could see the light streaming through the ceiling for the first time, and it exposed the flawed narrative in my head.

When I was around six years old, my family and I would visit my grandmother at her home in San Diego, California. To this day, that woman is one of the most domesticated women I know. She cooked. She cleaned. She did the laundry. She gardened. She baked hot cross buns and was the definition of a domesticated woman in my book. For a girl who barely knows how to iron, I find my grandmother a true woman of her time. One thing she took pride in, like most women raised in the 1930s, was acting like a lady.

About every few months, my parents would leave my brother and me with our grandmother so they could have some time to themselves. While my grandma had plenty of toys we could play with and videos to watch, I was often brutally bored. Maybe it's my borderline ADD or my anxious energy, but I honestly dreaded the days I spent watering her garden or finding unexpected moth balls in the bathroom. So, in true Sarah fashion, I would wrestle with my brother.

There we were, pulling hair, throwing elbows, yelling as if we were luchadores in Jack Black's *Nacho Libre*. Just as I'm having the time of my life, attempting to throw my older brother over my shoulder, I hear that haunting phrase:

"Sarah, stop that. Act like a lady."

Even six-year-old Sarah wanted to fight back. *Why do I have to act like a lady? I'm six!* I thought. I remember feeling frustrated and confused, especially when my brother did not get the same condemnation.

This demand to "act like a lady" has always rubbed me the wrong way. Something about it makes me feel like I'm being trapped in my own skin, like I'm being restricted and restrained. It's as if I'm being tied down to a chair, unable to move or escape.

When I was eighteen years old, I remember sitting down in my doctor's office after getting into a pretty bad tubing accident. I broke my ribs and got a concussion, making it extremely difficult to breathe and leaving me feeling incapacitated. As an incredibly active girl, I spent most of my days engaging in some sort of exercise. Whether walking, swimming, or hiking, I am an incredibly energetic person to say the least, and I love to expel that energy in the form of working out. However, when I asked my doctor what I was supposed to do to expedite my healing process after my injury, she said a statement that stuck with me: "Sit there and look pretty."

Was she serious? I was supposed to sit my ass on my couch in the middle of summer and just exist? Nothing sounded worse to me. While I understand resting comes with healing, the "look pretty" statement really left a bad taste in my mouth. Why couldn't I sit there and look ugly, look average, or anything in between? Why was it always pretty?

It seems as if, growing up, young girls are taught to be one way and one way only.

Be a lady, they say. Be polite, they say. Be kind. Look presentable. Don't question. Shut your mouth. You're being too loud.

It's as if these words have run through my mind since the first moment I could consciously remember. Toying with my mind and eroding away at who I truly am, these phrases like "act like a lady" or "sit there and look pretty" paint young women as one-dimensional characters. These expectations confine women to boxes and constrain them from putting their hands in multiple baskets, so to speak.

In her world-renowned TED Talk, "The Danger of a Single Story," Chimamanda Ngozi Adichie talks of how literature and other narratives have an incredible way of influencing our thoughts and ideas of the world around us. After growing up in a middle-class Nigerian household, Chimamanda attended college in the States. To her surprise, her roommate asked her to play some of her favorite "tribal music" for her. Chimamanda laughed as she told this story and said her new roommate was "consequently very disappointed when [she] produced [her] tape of Mariah Carey" (Adichie, 4:25).

But was it really the roommate's fault for thinking this way? After all, in the United States at least, Africa is commonly known as poor, rural, and uncivilized. Many people see Africa as one country, even though it is a continent with multiple languages and cultures. But many of the narratives we listen to and learn growing up seem to be the same single narrative repeatedly, reaffirming our faulty beliefs about people, places, and problems. We are fed the lie that if you are not in, then you are out. If you can't be popular, you are simply unpopular. If you're not considered pretty, then you are ugly. It's always one or the other, always one dimension rather than multiple.

As women, we are taught not to be too much, act out too much, or say too much. It's not what the "it girls" do. Doing so would inherently cause us to become our own worst enemy, right?

Wrong.

We women become our own worst enemies when we deny ourselves. We become our own worst enemies when we say yes to sitting back and watching life happen before our very own eyes, rather than jumping in the driver's seat and taking the wheel of our divinely ordained lives.

In all honesty, I've felt constricted and constrained for most of my life. In college, I tried to play the role of the "cute, blonde" girl, the role of the "easy-going, fun-loving" girl. I tried to act like the "I have it all together and everyone loves me" girl. I smiled when I needed to. I dressed in clothes that were considered trendy, rather than clothes I wanted to wear. I exercised way too much because I thought being skinny was the only way guys would like me.

It was exhausting. It was painful. It broke down my soul with every disingenuous interaction. I unconsciously put myself in a box because that's what I thought I had to do. That's what everyone would want, what I was taught to do.

Glennon Doyle, New York Times Bestseller and author of *Untamed*, once said, "We were taught to believe that who we are in our natural state is bad and dangerous. They convinced us to be afraid of ourselves. So, we do not honor our own bodies, curiosity, hunger, judgment, experience, or ambition. Instead, we lock away our true selves. Women who are best at this disappearing act earn the highest praise: She is so selfless. . . . The epitome of womanhood is to lose one's self completely . . . because a very effective way to control women is to convince women to control themselves" (Doyle, 2020).

Women are taught to be simple, not complex—one-dimensional, not multi-faceted. We are taught to lock up and abandon our truest selves, to shun our multi-faceted nature and conform to what society expects us to be. This ideology has suffocated women for years, making us feel like imposters. We no longer feel like we can live out our fullest expression without fear of being ridiculed. We spend years and years trying to fit in boxes we were never meant to squeeze into. We become something we are not, and we are left feeling like frauds.

But aren't we the frauds when we have abandoned ourselves for a more manicured version of ourselves? Who is really to blame—society or us?

The term "imposter syndrome" was first coined back in 1978 by American psychologists Pauline Clance and Suzanne Imes, and essentially means one does not feel deserving of something, or feels like a fraud for accomplishing or achieving something (Bennett, 2021). According to a review article published in the *International Journal of Behavioral Science*, about 70 percent of people experience imposter syndrome at one point or another in their lives (Abrams, 2018). According to Brian Daniel Norton, a psychotherapist and executive coach in New York, "women, women of colour (sic), especially Black women, as well as the LGBTQ community are most at risk" of developing imposter syndrome because these groups are disproportionally represented, especially in the workplace (Nance-Nash, 2020).

In KPMG's 2020 edition of *Advancing the Future of Women in Business: A KPMG Women's Leadership Summit Report*—which helps to demystify imposter syndrome in the world of executive women—the study found the number one power gap between men and women in the workplace was that women were unable to recognize their talents, abilities, and gifts compared to men. Unfortunately, for many women, imposter syndrome seems to follow them everywhere (KPMG Study Finds 75 percent Have Experienced Imposter Syndrome, 2020).

Imposter syndrome seems to ebb and flow in and out of our lives with each passing season. With each wave of imposter syndrome comes the reevaluation of who you are at your very core. I think we know who we are at our core being, but we are all surrounded by too many distractions and confronted with crippling mental noise, whether that be social media, our parents' thoughts, or our friends' opinions.

I think sometimes we try hard to run away from our past selves. We run and jump and dodge over any potential threat, away from our calling, away from our past, and away from our impending future. Right when we think we have escaped whatever we were running away from, right when we think we have finally perfected our act, right when we think we finally escaped ourselves, we trip and fall. We are once again right back where we started. It can seem like a never-ending cycle for some. It's as if we can spend a lifetime trying to be something we're not or something we would rather be, but the people around us or our subconscious thoughts are always three steps ahead, waiting for us to fall. It's almost as if they are there to remind us of who we really are or who we ought to be.

This cycle of running away from our past selves and falling into them once again can feel stifling and exhausting. From personal experience, I have spent months upon months becoming a better version of myself, only to be reminded of who I once was.

At the start of 2019, I made the promise to myself that I would change my life and outlook for the better. I had just come back from studying abroad in Italy, I was still concussed, anxious, and depressed, and I was already dreading graduation (it was still a year and a half away, but I often like to get ahead of myself). To put it lightly, I felt like a mess.

So, during my first month of 2019 at home in Arizona, I threw myself into anything and everything that would "heal" me. To me, that meant no drinking, no boys, getting over eight hours of sleep every night, daily exercise, journaling, listening to sermons and praying (a lot!), and daily affirmations. After a month of healthy living, I could already notice a difference. I was happy, lighter, and a lot less stressed and anxious. My headaches had begun to go away slowly but surely, and it was during this time I started to evolve into the person I truly wanted to be. For me, that meant becoming the person I knew I always was. I began to stop caring what others would think. I started doing triathlons, and it turns out I'm pretty freaking good at them! When I went out to the bars, I no longer sought the validation from subpar frat boys. Instead, I focused on just having a good time with my friends. I started to be more vocal regarding my views on all topics from politics to religion to sexual assault and mental health. I even started a podcast, which has since grown to be one of the best things I've ever done with my life besides writing this book.

Though I still had my struggles and still carried some baggage from the past with me (as we all do), I learned to shed most of that weight and become someone I really freaking loved. But in 2020 when I decided to go to therapy to further my personal journey, I experienced incredible waves of anger and frustration as I began to talk and work through the events of my past with my therapist. From my childhood to my sexual assaults to my anxiety, it felt as if tsunami waves of emotions rolled over me, leaving me completely crippled and distraught. I think often people believe therapy will be this liberating and freeing experience where you just talk about your "feelings" and frustrations from the day. While it is a very liberating and freeing experience, therapy is very taxing and emotional. You uncover why you are the way you are. You talk about the moments in your life you have tried so hard to push deep down. You are focused on remembering all of the hurt and pain you have tried so hard to forget.

So, while I was going through this experience, coupled with my impending graduation, I unfairly took out my unresolved anger and frustration on the people I loved. I will not convey the details of this story in full to respect the privacy of the people involved, but I will say both sides said extremely hurtful things, including myself.

Sometimes, even the people we love the most will come back to remind us we are frauds—even if they don't really mean it. They'll say the work we did to better ourselves was just an illusion. They'll say, "Oh, that's cute," as they scoff and walk away.

Sometimes those naysayers are ourselves. The voice in our heads tell us our devotion to our grueling, painstaking journey to a more beautified version of our interior selves was for nothing. That voice declares we are not allowed to make mistakes and backtrack from time to time, and says our work is something that can wither away and disintegrate at any moment.

But here's the thing: we can't let these lies destroy us. These are the lies from the enemy. Little, insignificant lies that, for some reason, we attribute complete and utter truth to. We allow our lack of confidence in ourselves to dictate what we believe, but I think we've been conditioned to think this way, to shove ourselves into these boxes and be one-dimensional, to fit the mold.

Did you know women often exhibit a lot less confidence than men? There are actually scientific studies on confidence comparing men and women, and the jury is in! In every study, every blog, and every article I could find, each and every expert was saying the same things—men are the confident ones and are more likely to overstate their results. According to one study I found, the researchers claimed the lack of women in leadership positions was due to the fact men were simply more confident compared to women. Though the lack of female representation in leadership is not entirely due to our lack of confidence, it definitely doesn't help. As mentioned earlier, women and other minority groups experience imposter syndrome at an alarmingly disproportionate rate, creating a less than favorable environment for them in their professional and personal lives (McGregor, 2011).

I've spent many years of my life feeling as if I was an imposter or as if I have to remain in my one-dimensional box. Have you experienced this, too? Maybe you've had people come into your life, whether it be family, a friend, a boss, or stranger on the internet, and tell you that you are not who you think you are. They try to remind you of all your faults. They try to point out where the pieces don't match up and where you're most likely to fall. They try to stir up insecurities that are within all of us, eagerly waiting for us to fail. Sometimes, it doesn't matter just how hard we've worked to become something or someone else. At the end of the day, we are all reminded we are frauds at one time or another.

So how do you overcome this feeling of being a fraud or imposter? How can you give yourself permission to break outside of the box and be multi-faceted, as you were created to be?

There can be a million answers to these questions, but I will give you one:

Separate the facts from feelings.

I once heard someone say that not every thought we have is true. While that is obvious to some, my mind was blown. I never truly thought about it that way. Too often, we allow these false thoughts to dictate how we feel. Our thoughts tell us we are inadequate, so we feel inadequate. Our thoughts tell us we are a fraud, so we feel like a fraud. Our thoughts tell us we will never be enough, so be believe that and take those negative feelings on. But we are not our feelings, we simply experience them. And we are allowed to let the facts speak for themselves (Young, 2021).

I'm a firm believer that every single person placed on this earth was created to be different. There is no one like you, no one with your exact smile, no one with your exact thoughts, and no one with your exact experiences. We are all unique in our own way.

When you understand this fact, you begin to separate facts from feelings. You might feel like you never fit in, but you were never really made to. You might feel like you will never be enough, but you were created with a divine sense of wholeness—one only you can fully embody. By separating your feelings from the facts, you begin to allow yourself space to grow and prosper. You begin to allow yourself to flow into new dimensions rather than being suffocated in your previous one.

It's cliche, but you are allowed to be you, the you who experiences five different emotions at once. The you who feels so much love yet so much grief, the you who wants to experience so much life, yet so desperately wants to be left alone. The you who feels as though they are finally getting a grip on life, yet has absolutely nothing figured out.

Give yourself permission to show up as you are. You are not a fraud. You are not an imposter. You are just you, and that is more than enough.

CHAPTER TWO

CULTURAL PRESSURES

Have you ever watched *My Big Fat Greek Wedding*? It's a fabulous movie, if you haven't already seen it. For my family, it was and is to this day one of our favorites for many reasons.

My mom is half Greek, and my great-grandfather came over to the US from Greece with nothing but a third-grade education in hopes of pursuing the American Dream. From my personal experience, Greek people take a lot of pride purely in being Greek, no matter what percentage you are. For my family, it's no different. Our favorite food is lamb, we attend Phoenix's Greek festival every year, and we listen to Greek music regularly. We love being Greek!

Chances are, you can define yourself in a cultural sense, whatever way that may be. Maybe you eat certain foods, talk a certain way, or enjoy doing certain activities. Maybe you practice a certain religion or have certain beliefs directly tied to your culture. Whatever your cultural practices are, these things have shaped you into the person you are today and affect how you think about yourself and the world around you.

For Lauren Lapid, a first-generation Filipino woman, cultural identity is something that has influenced her outlook and perspective on the world from the very beginning.

"It's interesting because when I think about defining myself, being a first-generation Asian American is probably at the top of my list," Lauren said. "There are a lot of cultural gaps I feel I've had to come to terms with between me, between my family in the Philippines, and between my parents. . . . We are products of our society, and so I've had to come to terms with kinds of the expectations my mom has had for my sister and for me and for our futures."

Growing up, Lauren was incredibly artistic. But Lauren's parents always thought of her artistic hobbies as just that—a hobby. So, despite her interest in the arts, Lauren's parents were adamant she and her sister both enter the STEM field. She would either work in the medical field or as a lawyer, and those fields, her parents believed, were the only two acceptable industries one could find success in.

As the youngest child in the family, Lauren often reminisced about being the boundary breaker of the family. "In my case," Lauren explained, "my sister majored in biology, was very involved in school, and was picture perfect—or as it seemed in my parents' eyes." On the other hand, Lauren deemed herself the "creative black sheep" of the family. "Living in [her sister's] shadow, knowing what her parents expected, and having a daughter who fit what they expected," Lauren never quite felt like she fit it. "There was so much mental noise because every little thing I did, I wondered, 'Will this make my parents proud, or will this piss them off?'" She felt as if she was walking on eggshells.

Despite her differences and desires to break her cultural and traditional mold, Lauren still tried her best in school to get high marks and threw herself into extracurricular activities like speed skating. "I was a speed skater for most of my life, and six out of seven days a week, I was with my team and with my coach," Lauren said proudly. Most speed skaters dream of reaching the sport's pinnacle of success: the Olympics. For Lauren, it was no different.

But as high school went on, Lauren's grades started to slip, and with college applications right around the corner, she had to make an incredibly tough decision. "When I had to quit [speed skating] my junior year, I was lost, I was so angry, and I felt like such a failure in a sense. I had gotten to the age where my friends and my peers were going to be the on next Olympic team. I know people right now who are qualifying for the Olympics, and I'm so stoked to share their bond. But it feels like I'm watching them through the lens of like, another life."

With Lauren's tough decision came a lot of extra free time and a dark depression. She began to spiral. "I was depressed for a long time. I didn't care about anything because I suddenly had a ton of free time. Before, I would be up at 4:00 a.m., and I'd be at the rink by 5:30 a.m." But now, it was a different story. The rebellious part of Lauren came out in full swing. Lauren thought, "If I'm going to have to go to college, I'm going to do it on my own terms, and I'm going to be an art major."

While Lauren's decision made her feel good about herself, her parents felt another way. "There is a period for months where my parents and I just didn't speak because they were so angry at me for not following what they wanted." But despite her parents' qualms, Lauren and her parents eventually found common ground when she agreed to attend a four-year college rather than a traditional art school—just in case she changed her mind about her major.

At school at George Mason University, Lauren received high marks in all her design classes, and in the summer between her freshman and sophomore year, she got the opportunity of a lifetime. Lauren accepted a summer internship at Adobe, and to Lauren's surprise and satisfaction, her parents finally began to turn around. As a largely recognized tech company, Adobe provided Lauren with the opportunity to learn more about her craft and allowed her parents to realize the graphic design industry was a lucrative industry.

After four years fighting for her own path, Lauren graduated as a graphic design major and valedictorian of her class. "I had finally felt like I'd made my parents proud by the end of college. My parents were like, 'My daughter's a graphic designer! She does this!' I was like, 'You guys never would have said this ten years ago.'" It's funny how our memory conveniently fails us from time to time.

But, while it might seem like Lauren was finally in the clear, there was one more major obstacle standing in her way: the post-graduation job hunt. Getting a job post-graduation is no easy task; I can personally attest to this. For Lauren, it was no different. "I didn't have a full-time offer, and I felt like a fool, like such an imposter," Lauren said with a sigh, "because for four years, I was that girl who always had the job, always had her shit together." Quickly, her parents reverted back to their old viewpoint and "all the toxicity just resurfaced."

However, Lauren did receive one offer for a fellowship in New York City for a PR agency. So, for the next ten weeks, Lauren hustled harder than she ever had before. She networked. She shook hands with the bigwigs of NYC. By the end of those two and a half months in the city, Lauren landed a job at Condé Nast—making both Lauren and her parents incredibly proud.

While Lauren's story of staying true to herself and her personal identity is inspirational, it is also incredibly common for women of any cultural background. Whether you come from a white, Black, Asian, Latino, Indigenous, or mixed background, certain cultural ideologies and beliefs were presented to you from a young age and have shaped what you believe you can and can't do with your life. I personally know many other friends who have fought hard to keep their dream of being a public health worker or filmmaker alive, despite what their parents and cultural norms desired for them merely because they are women.

For Dina Kaur, a mental health reporter at *The State News*, growing up as a young woman in an Indian household had a slew of challenges. From expectations around marriage, appearances, and careers, Dina struggled with the cultural pressures placed upon her. She struggled with the idea that she was meant to be "someone's wife," and the idea that she had to pursue a career that was "practical" to be successful.

Navigating her own cultural pressures caused her to redefine herself by her own standards, rather than purely a cultural one (Kaur and Daniel, 2021).

In Indian culture, a ninety-year-old grandmother will continue to cook and clean up after the adult men of the household, even if she is weak and tired. In Mexican culture, many women are taught how to do household chores while their male siblings are taught none of these things. In Korean culture, some parents will only allow their daughters to play piano because it is deemed "more suitable for girls" (Andrews, 2020).

While I do not wish to reduce these cultural practices down to a single sentence with the examples above, as each and every culture is layered and dynamic, these examples do exemplify common cultural beliefs and traditions in certain cultures regarding women. These beliefs and traditions are neither good nor bad, but rather how a cultural community chooses to operate. However, when cultural practices and traditions begin to impede women's rights, that's when the conversation gets tricky.

Dr. Shawn Andrews is a gender expert who has spent a lifetime talking to individuals and conducting research about how gender effects identity. "We've been socialized," she says, "according to our gender." Socialization, or "the process of learning to behave in a way that is acceptable to society," allows us to put different things and actions into different boxes. For example, a girl plays with dolls and a boy plays with trucks. As we grow up and carry on with our lives, these narratives continue to infiltrate our day-to-day actions, especially for certain cultural communities (Andrews, 2020).

Culture has a huge impact on how we view life and ourselves. Unfortunately, many cultures—including American culture—are inundated with gender-biases, allowing for many double standards to take place. According to Dr. Andrews, "[g]ender roles at home can and should be blurred." In addition, she believes "[w]e should also be aware of cultural inconsistencies in how we treat girls and boys and the messages we are sending our daughters." By having more gender-neutral practices, women might have a greater ability and freedom to choose their own path and be confident in doing so, and I couldn't agree more (Andrews, 2020).

However, I need to acknowledge both my views and Dr. Andrew's views on this matter are rather individualistic. In America and many Western cultures, autonomy over yourself and your future is considered essential for living a happy, healthy, and whole life. Thus, we tend to have an individualistic mindset when it comes to how our decisions will affect us personally. For me, I was raised by entrepreneurial parents who told me if I ever wanted to achieve a certain level of greatness, I'd have to be willing to walk the road less traveled and not follow the pack.

But in other cultures, there tends to be a different narrative. Many Asian and Hispanic cultures have more of a collectivist mindset, which informs their cultural norms and expectations. If you came from a culturally collectivist background, such as Latin, Asian, African, and Mediterranean cultures, chances are you have been taught to focus on a common goal, rather than an individual pursuit. Or perhaps you were taught that group loyalty takes the cake and it is best to make decisions with the whole group in mind. But despite having a collectivist mindset, I'm a firm believer that one can honor her culture while staying true to herself (Cherry, 2021).

While I acknowledge I never grew up with a collectivist household, both Lauren's and Dina's stories show where one can honor their own culture while forging their own path. For Lauren, forging her own path while honoring her Filipino culture was incredibly challenging, but empowering. The mental noise and various distractions from family and friends during this time of growth and reckoning might seem too heavy to handle at first. But, in Lauren's case, helping her parents redefine how they saw success allowed Lauren to honor herself while keeping her Filipino heritage alive.

For Dina, she will never stop being proud of her cultural upbringing, even though she now incorporates Western values into her own ideology. She states:

> While there are many things about Indian culture that scream "NO" there are also things that I wouldn't change.... Having multiple layered identities as a woman of color, I face many different struggles, some that my white friends may not associate with or deal with. I'm more hopeful that my culture adapts with me as I'm learning to adapt within a Western society. I am proud of my culture and where my family comes from. I know I strive to set an example and be a strong Indian woman.

As women, we can honor our cultural upbringings while pressing forward into new territory. As women, we can become that doctor, artist, or businesswoman while honoring the place where we once were. As women, we are allowed to show up as we are while celebrating the culture that set our primary foundation into place.

CHAPTER THREE

YOUR LIMITING BELIEFS ARE LIMITING YOU IN MORE WAYS THAN ONE

—

I sat there on the edge of my bed. My eyes closed, and my hands were on my chest.
Inhale. Big breath in.
Exhale. Big breath out.

I simultaneously began to tap my chest and think of a time where I felt alone. To be honest, I thought this was all a little weird, but I assumed my therapist knew what she was doing. I mean, after all, I was paying her the big bucks to help me with all my issues.

So, I sat there tapping my chest and thinking of a time when I was in sixth grade. I was horrendously bullied that year. Every day, I would come home crying to my mom, telling her they called me *weird* yet again. I was never popular. I was never skinny. I wasn't one of those girls who was super girly and wore bows in her hair. I was just Sarah and was confused about this damn thing called life.

Then came that not-so-beloved memory. I remember it like it was yesterday. Sitting in the second row in the classroom, I was busy chatting up a storm with my classmates as our teacher was next door collecting the materials for the day. Earlier that day, I was at my locker with a classmate—let's call her Stephanie. Stephanie had this fabulous brown, curly hair she always threw back in a ponytail. It was long and bouncy, and you could tell she definitely knew how to deep condition. As I was with Stephanie by the lockers, I looked over and stroked her hair like I had always done. Then, I proceeded to tell her that her hair had the consistency of chocolate pudding. Yes, I told one of my classmates repeatedly her hair was like some subpar dessert you find in the refrigerated section of any major grocery store.

I knew she hated it when I told her that. But frankly, I didn't like Stephanie, and she didn't like me. The feeling was mutual. Stephanie would bully me every day in sixth grade. She called me weird and a whole host of other hurtful names. She and the other girls would exclude me from most things. I was never allowed to join in on their basketball or volleyball games. I was always picked last for kickball. I felt like I spent most of my childhood in the background, invisible and lonely, frustrated by the lack of attention and desperate to find my way out of the shadows. It was from an incredibly young age that I could feel myself wanting to break free from this facade that encompassed my very being. Out of my innocent angst, I would say her hair looked like pudding. Amateur move, I know, but I was never good at comebacks.

So, this day did not seem different from any other. She called me weird. I said her hair looked like pudding. But today, something different happened. My teacher had stepped out of the classroom for only a moment, and Stephanie, sitting in the row in front of me, stood up and announced, "Sarah, you are a freak, and no one likes you." The room fell silent. I vaguely remember some of my classmates telling her that was not nice, but it didn't matter at this point. My ego was already deflated, and I began to shrink back into myself.

I skipped school the next day. I couldn't face them anymore. I was broken and sad. I was an outcast and knew I didn't fit in.

Now, I don't blame them for making fun of me. In all honesty, I was a *really* weird kid. I went around telling everyone I had an imaginary friend named Zebo. He was a zebra who sang songs and did other weird things like that. Here's the kicker: I didn't even believe in Zebo. I just told everyone I had an imaginary friend because I wanted to spice things up a bit. I found the people at my school to be incredibly boring. They all fit into the same mold, the kind where you do what you're told and follow the pack.

I, for one, did not fit that mold. So, to make it clear to everyone I was not a part of their club, I knowingly made myself "the weird girl." But hey, someone had to keep this place interesting. Everyone else was as dry as toast. I was the rosemary focaccia in the land of Wonder Bread.

Though I knowingly made myself the outsider, I was hoping one day I'd be welcomed with open arms and suddenly have a million friends. I was hoping I would be popular for once, but that never happened. While I knew my actions were making me stand out, all I wanted to do was fit in. I both despised the in-crowd and yet wanted to be a part of it desperately. I was standing on the outside staring in. I wanted to be known. I wanted to be seen.

Each day that I came home crying to my mom, I questioned if I would ever fit in. Did I even really matter? I shuttered and prayed to God to save me from this mess.

So, there I am, sitting on my bed at twenty-three years old, tapping my chest and thinking of how my childhood bullies made me want to die.

"What feelings are coming up?" my therapist asked. "What is something you deem to be true?"

"That I was lonely? Yeah, lonely." I tried to convince myself that was the core belief about myself, that I would always be alone. She told me to think about it some more, and our session ended.

During this time, the fear of coronavirus was quickly grabbing hold of the world. Schools were shut down. A work-from-home order was put in place. To my biggest dismay, the beaches were closed—a true tragedy. Now, I was forced to walk the alleyways of Mission Beach. It was not the most scenic walk, if you ask me. The alleyways are covered with trash, the crime rate is fairly high, and it smells. Not the most ideal place when you're looking to take a nice walk. Nevertheless, I was itching to get out of my house during those early days of quarantine. So, I would go on my daily five-mile walks and talk to God.

Later that week after my therapy session, I was thinking about what she said. Did I really think my main problem in life was I'd be forever lonely? No. That wasn't 100 percent accurate. I racked my brain for my truth. Sanding on the corner of Pacific Beach Drive and Ingraham, my truth hit me like a ton of bricks. *I am not seen.*

In that very moment, every failed relationship, every hurt, and every painful memory could be tied to this one belief. I understood the reason why I tend to be slightly obnoxious in certain settings. I understood why I had an eating disorder. I understood why I had let every attractive asshole walk all over me. I understood why my family environment sometimes causes me to become an explosive volcano from time to time, able to erupt at any second of the day. It was because I felt like no one saw me for me.

It sounds dramatic, but it's true. I had built my entire life off the idea that no one ever noticed me. I had felt unimportant, dismissed, and rejected by many people in my life. Every lie I had told myself, like the lie that no guy would ever notice me or the lie that I would never be someone of importance, was built upon the fact I felt like I was invisible to most of the human population.

My truth washed over me like a title wave. I thought, *Huh, maybe this therapist does know what she's talking about.*

We all have unrealized thoughts and ideas about ourselves, and these unrealized thoughts and ideas are often subconscious. They were always there to begin with, we just never take the time to explore them. This is due to the fact that too many of us spend so much time distracting ourselves. We push the feelings away and store them in theoretical compartments in our heads. We run away from our past and can't seem to understand why we act out or why we feel a certain way when life gets hectic in the present. Our limiting beliefs and the way we talk to ourselves, cope with our problems, and show up in our daily lives all come back to one core thing: what we believe about ourselves.

Not long after my epiphany, I was able to sit down with Haley Hoffman Smith to record an episode all about manifestation for my podcast. Haley—a TikTok sensation, manifestation coach, motivational speaker, and author—preaches the importance of breaking past our internal boundaries and uncovering old belief systems inhibiting us from reaching our fullest potential. During the episode, we talked about how limiting beliefs often get in the way of accomplishing our dreams, and that's when Haley said something that struck me: "You can't have both at the same time. You can't believe something about the world that you've [believed for so long] and invite an experience that's completely contrary to that belief" (Hoffman Smith, 22.30).

I think often we spend so much time trying to accomplish something, trying to accomplish our dreams, trying to have that perfect relationship, or trying to land that big job, but we always seem to fall short. While obvious circumstances and other logistics are at play, our limiting beliefs are a huge player in this game. Maybe you can't have that perfect relationship because you really believe you don't deserve respect. Maybe you can't land that dream job of yours and bomb the interview because you simply don't believe you are competent. Maybe you're afraid of walking into a room of strangers not because they won't like you, but because long ago you developed the belief that you were never good enough, not even for yourself.

When it comes to the toxic relationship you're in, maybe you've been wired to find comfort in those types of relationships because they are the prominent types of relationships in your life, and that's what you've been repeatedly exposed to. The belief that you can't ever be the CEO of a company may come from you telling yourself that you're not good enough and believing a negative subconscious narrative of your life.

We spend so much time blaming others for things when we really should take more responsibility. Like Haley said, "If you aren't willing to go completely deep and look at the parts of yourself that are really scary to look at or parts of your past, you're not going to be able to receive manifestations" or achieve what you set out to do (Hoffman Smith, 22.30).

But let's get real: who really wants to spend the time leaning into parts of their painful past? Who wants to talk about that time they were left in shambles, in complete distress, and utterly broken? I sure don't. But I do it anyways because I've decided my dreams are far too important for my broken past to get in the way.

I think your dreams deserve the same respect. You don't have to keep repeating cycles you don't want to be in. It's up to you and your brain.

CHANGE YOUR BRAIN, CHANGE YOUR LIFE

It turns out, you can actually change your brain with how you think. Your brain is changing at this very moment as you are reading my words. With every interaction, every conversation, and every experience, your brain's neuroplasticity— or your brain's "ability to modify, change, and adapt both structure and function throughout life and in response to experience" —is constantly evolving (Patrice Voss, et al. 2017). By positively changing our thought structure and function of our brains, research shows changing thoughts through the use of the brain's neuroplasticity can help to "treat eating disorders, prevent cancer, lower our risk of dementia by 60 percent, and help us discover our 'true essence of joy and peace'" (Will Storr, 2015).

So to counteract these thought processes, you must actively make changes in your life. Adrienne Finch, a YouTuber, Tik-Tok sensation, and podcast host of *Self-Made Mastery*, told me during an interview, "It's those small little things that end up rewiring our brains" (Finch, 19.30). It's the daily affirmations, the visualization of a better future, and the active little changes in our everyday lives. These are the things that can make or break us, and these are things that can change our brain for the better or the worse.

Adrienne went on to say, "That's where the most progress will be made, is when you do like, little actions every single day—because honestly, we give ourselves sometimes too much credit. It's really hard for us to make a major change in our lifestyle" (Finch, 19.30).

Have you ever jumped into something you thought you were ready for, but really weren't? A great example of this is dating. If you have just gotten out of a toxic relationship and then jumped straight into a healthy relationship, you might have gotten the "ick." The "ick" is a similar feeling to annoyance. It's when every single thing that person does appalls you.

They text you good morning. *Ick.*
They send you flowers. *Ick.*
They say "I love you." *Major Ick.*

But chances are, you're probably just disgusted by this behavior because you are not used to it due to your previous relationship. Your brain is simply not used to this kind of loving treatment, so you push that person away.

That's why it starts with baby steps first. You must slowly change your thoughts, slowly change your habits, and slowly change how you show up bit by bit. For me, baby steps looked like telling myself I was good enough, despite what other people did or didn't say about me. Baby steps looked like saying daily affirmations and praying. Baby steps looked like gaining confidence through engaging in purposeful work, rather than working for superficial reasons. Baby steps might look different for you, and that's okay! The point is to change your brain and thoughts one day at a time. You're never going to be an overnight success story, and that's more than okay. No one else is either, despite what the media tries to tell you.

While the work isn't pretty or cute, I have set out to continually work to dig through the pile of messy lies etched deep within my mind. Because at the end of the day, I refuse to give life to the lie that caused me so much hurt and pain throughout the course of my life.

I want you to dig out those lies, too. Dig out the lies that have caused you immense emotional pain, that made you think that you are not good enough, that said you are not loved. Those lies are liars, and they don't deserve space anymore.

Now get your shovel and start digging. I promise it's not as scary as you think.

CHAPTER FOUR

REDEFINING BEAUTY ON YOUR OWN TERMS

Gap-toothed. Practically albino. Prepubescent boobs.

Yes, from what my memory and my childhood pictures tell me, I had a big gap in between my two front teeth, was whiter than Wonder Bread, and went through puberty starting in the third grade.

Let's just say, my childhood was not my "prime time" in terms of looks. While the other girls at school had absolutely zero ounces of body fat on them, I seemed to still carry most of my baby fat on me. To say I was chubby was an understatement. To give you more context, I am basically now the same weight I was in the sixth grade, only taller.

As much as I wish I could say I was blissfully unaware of my body and how others viewed it, I was teased and bullied about my weight since I was four years old. Yes, since I was four—and I remember the moment when I was first teased about my weight like it was yesterday.

It was a hot Arizona summer day, and my best friend at the time and I were having a playdate at her house. We were pretending to be mermaids as we launched ourselves from one end of the pool to the other. Diving through pool hoops and noodles, I remember that moment in time blissfully, but the moment to come was a different story.

After hours of playing in the pool, my mom was on her way to pick me up, so I rushed inside and began to change out of my one piece. Little children, in my opinion, are notorious for being very liberal with how they choose to clothe themselves. I was no different. There I stood, door open, directly facing the hallway as I began to undress. Just as my swimsuit hit the floor and I stood there completely naked, my friend walked by, looked me straight in the eyes, and told me, "You're fat." Then she walked away laughing.

That was the first time I ever felt shame. It's funny how at such an early age, we begin to be taught what is "good" and what is "bad." Skinny is good. Fat is bad. Because I was now "fat," I was bad.

Later that night, I remember pressing my face into my mom's chest as tears streamed down my cheeks. She did everything a good mom is supposed to do. She consoled me, wiped away my tears, and told me I was beautiful. But I didn't believe it. This was a memory I had carried with me for most of my life, and as a teenager, this was the memory that stayed at the top of mind as I drove myself into dangerous behaviors.

By seventeen years old, I was in the trenches of dealing with anorexia, orthorexia (the obsession with healthy or clean eating), and binge eating. This gnarly combination is one that almost took my life.

I hated getting ready for school every morning because that meant I had to stare in the mirror and look at myself. It was a reminder that I would never look like one of those models I would see on Instagram. I spent hours and hours on end after school looking at Victoria Secret models and other thin women dressed in bikinis and revealing clothing. I had convinced myself I was so incredibly ugly no one could possibly ever love me—all because I didn't have the "ideal" body type.

Looking back, I think social media amplified my insecurities to the point of devastation. The constant visuals on my screen of women that society deemed "pretty" was a reminder that I did not live up to that standard. For many young girls and women, the story is the same.

I recently sat down with Megan Maas—an associate professor at Michigan State University, a developmental psychologist, and an expert in female adolescent sexual development—to talk about the mental and emotional effects social media has played in the development of young women. Maas confirmed anxiety, mental illness, suicide, and self-harm have increased exponentially in the past decade when comparing this statistic to decades past. Particularly, studies have shown a much higher spike in anxiety and depression among young women, rather than young men. This spike in mental illness is attributed to the popularization of social media.

Maas mentioned studies show there is a rise in self-objectification since the internet and social media era began. "We do know that there are things like self-objectification, where you are thinking of yourself more in terms of how you look instead of how you feel, how you think, and how you experience the world." Maas went on to state some young women and girls say this state of self-objectification feels as if they are seeing themselves from an outside perspective.

In addition, the use of editing software has also become popularized over the years as Instagram and other picture-sharing platforms have gained traction. As a result, "adolescent girls who do a lot of selfie editing, take a lot of selfies, and post mostly edited pictures have a much higher rate of anxiety and depression compared to the girls who don't use the photo-editing softwares." It would make sense for mental illness to be directly correlated to this misuse of social media. We've created an environment of perfectly curated photos and feeds that make it difficult to separate fantasy from reality.

When asked about how social media and the constant stimulation of perfectly curated photos affect young women, Maas noted these images on social media are portraying a new narrative to women: that if they present a hot, sexy, stylish, beautiful, or mysterious persona online, this persona can gain notoriety of some sort, whether that means becoming an influencer or landing sponsorship deals. It's portraying the message that if they keep a "hot and sexy" outer appearance, they will get the attention and money they are looking for.

This constant striving for perfection can be debilitating. The portrayal on social media that women's bodies are merely an object rather than a living, breathing human reaffirms this false narrative that women are worthless and worth less if they don't live up to our society's definition of perfection.

For me, looking in the mirror brought me to tears almost every single time because it affirmed that I was far from "perfect." As high school went on and my eating disorder grew, thoughts of food and my body became all-consuming. I honestly don't remember much of high school. When you go through something traumatic, they say your mind tends to block out the memories associated with it. For me, this was no different. From what I do remember, the pain, depression, and anxiety drowned out everything else in life.

I pushed my friends away. I couldn't pay attention in my classes. I lost interest in anything and everything that didn't get me to my goal of being skinny. Eventually, my depression had gotten so crippling and so excruciating that living was a struggle.

Looking back, it breaks my heart that I heavily contemplated suicide. Typing those words doesn't even feel real. It feels like that time in my life was nothing but a never-ending nightmare. It feels like it was a past life because the woman writing these words right now would never even begin to question whether life is worth living. I love being alive, and I want to live my life to the fullest. But this detail is a part of my story. As open and vulnerable as I might seem, this detail is something I have shared with few. I honestly debated even including this detail in my book because I never would want anyone to think I am "crazy" or unstable. While it could be so easy for me to omit this detail from my story, I've decided to leave it in to show the true depths that obsessing over your body image can lead you. It's not pretty or cute or lovely, but it's real, and far too many women are allowing their looks to dictate their level of satisfaction in life.

According to the National Eating Disorder Association, over 70 percent of those with eating disorders will neglect treatment due to the stigma and shame attached to it. One out of every five people dealing with anorexia will die by suicide. Anorexia remains the deadliest mental illness to date (Pike, 2020). So, while my suicidal thoughts relating to my eating disorder might seem extreme to others, the reality is 20 percent of people dealing with this mental illness think the same way. That's 20 percent too great.

On my eighteenth birthday, a few months past that morbid experience and several months into therapy, I decided my birthday gift to myself would be recovery. While the road to recovery is never linear or easy, I can sit here today—despite all of the relapses and downturns—and tell you last night I ate all of the carbs and drank all of the wine. I don't feel an ounce of shame or regret. That's something I never thought I would say.

Yes, looking good can make you feel good, but everyone's definition of what "looks" good is relative. We are too often influenced by what society and social media deem as "beautiful" and "good." But here's a little news flash for you: much of our definition and beliefs relating to beauty are based on trends. Trends don't ever last, and if we try to keep up with trends, we'll inevitably and eventually fall behind. In Ancient Greece, beautiful women were seen as having a little extra weight on them. They had all the curves, and then some. During the Italian Renaissance and Victorian Era, women who were curvy, busty, and had thick hips were deemed the most beautiful. It wasn't really until the Roaring Twenties that being thin was popularized (BuzzFeedVideo, 2015). In today's day and age, our standards have changed once again. Figures like the Kardashians' are glorified for their voluptuous yet thin bodies.

So, you want to chase beauty? Good luck, because you'll never be able to obtain it if you go after what society says. It's ever-changing, dynamic, and fleeting. But if you begin to develop your own thoughts, opinions, and ideas of what beauty really is based on how you love and show up in this world, you'll be able to hit that mark every time.

I've learned to love how I look, even if I'm never going to be the girl with the completely flat stomach and skinny arms. Am I allowed to have some days where I have a bad body image? Absolutely, it's what makes me human. The key is to not ruminate and flip the narrative.

Now I absolutely love eating, and I don't feel guilty for indulging in excess sugar, carbs, or alcohol here and there—something I never would have imagined a few years ago. I learned to make peace with my body because it's the only one I will ever have. Most importantly, I learned my body and my looks are the least interesting things about me.

While we live in a beauty-obsessed society where perfectly curated pictures of beautiful women are the norm, I think it's time we begin to obsess about how we make others feel. Megan Maas's advice to younger women was to focus on the things that bring them joy. That could be yoga, art, horseback riding, hanging out with friends, you name it. But the point is this thing or activity that brings you joy "doesn't have to do with how you look and how others are going to be rating you." When you begin to find your self-worth in the things that make you a better human or the things that bring you a true sense of joy, you begin to block out what the world will say about you. You begin to develop your own sense of self—not based on society, but by your own standards. Let's get real, if you have a hobby or favorite activity, chances are you'll find yourself spending way less time on social media because you'll be dedicating your time to said hobby or activity. This, in turn, will help you to create a great foundation for your sense of identity.

While this piece of advice might seem simple on paper, it's harder to put into practice. Trust me, I would know. I honestly think it took me a solid twenty-three years to not completely base my own thoughts and opinions about myself off of what others say. It took me until my senior year of college to find something—besides exercise and beach walks—that brought me genuine joy. For me, these things are writing and podcasting. I love creating and articulating my thoughts and ideas through spoken and written word, and both are something I do for the sake of joy, not because others will think I am cool. In fact, some people might think the opposite now that I am more vocal about my passions, and that's okay. The point is I'm learning to fall in love with my own curiosity, my intelligence, and my eagerness to grow, rather than fall in love with my looks. I'm learning to shift my own personal narrative and place value on my own internal beauty rather than my external beauty.

Physical beauty is fine and all, but it sure as hell is never worth dying over. But beauty based on your own standards of how you love, how you show up, and what you find joy in? Now that's a game-changer.

CHAPTER FIVE

THE TOXIC TANGO

TikTok is literally a gift from the gods. I'm serious.

How could we have survived quarantine without it? How would we have spent our now lackluster Friday nights? By staring at a wall? By tweezing our eyebrows for the umpteenth time? By watching "cute moments" of your favorite TV characters on YouTube?

I'd like to take a hard pass on all of the above. That's why TikTok is revolutionary for our time. It has everything to keep our short attention spans engaged. From videos of Addison Rae dancing to fellow twenty-somethings complaining about how their ex-boyfriends are toxic, TikTok has something for everyone.

I have a long list of favorite TikTokers, but one of my favorites is Ally Yost. Her videos are bright, fun, heartfelt, and engaging, and oftentimes cover topics like self-worth, boundaries, and toxic relationships. Her videos are my favorite kind of content because they're relatable. Everyone—regardless of what gender or sexuality—can relate to being in a toxic or negative relationship.

Whether it's a familial, romantic, or platonic relationship, it can be hard to navigate toxic or incredibly negative relationships. Unless you've gone to therapy from a very young age or your parents were intentional about showing you what a healthy relationship looks like, navigating bumpy relationships is not something we learn in school. We aren't often taught how to set boundaries, express and communicate our emotions properly, and heal from any emotional trauma caused by relational issues. After all, these are key to a healthy relationship.

IT TAKES TWO TO BE TOXIC

I recently had a conversation with my friend Nadine Krill about our past relationships, per usual. Unfortunately, I feel as if we live in a society where everyone and everything has become "toxic." Toxic boyfriends, toxic girlfriends, toxic family members, toxic coworkers, and the list goes on.

As we were chatting on a Saturday morning, she said something that made me think: "It takes two to tango, but I like to put a little twist to the saying. It takes two to be toxic."

I initially laughed, but as I let a chuckle out, I thought hard for a minute.

Wait, have I been the toxic one? Are we all just toxic hot messes living in this perpetual cycle? If so, what does this mean for all relationships? No one is perfect, and everyone plays their own part. But how does this all play into our own ego when examining all our relationships gone wrong?

I, for one, have had many failed relationships with boys.

I've spent much of my time talking to my friends and therapist, telling them how this boy drank too much, that boy never listened, the other one only wanted to sleep with me. They always seemed to do something that crossed the line. But, in all honesty, I exhibited these behaviors myself. I drank too much with them. I ignored them when they ignored me. I played their games and pretended not to care.

I was doing the toxic tango all along.

During college, I ended a relationship a few days into our winter break, and I was reflecting on all that went wrong. While a part of me really did love him, I knew certain behaviors fell into my non-negotiable file. The heavy drinking, the partying, the lack of communication, and the lack of addressing issues of any kind were a few. Combine this all together, and you get a hot mess of a relationship. Don't get me wrong, I thoroughly enjoy having a few glasses of wine here and there, and I've taken my fair share of tequila shots before. But when drinking and partying take the front seat before my work, health, and wellness priorities, that's when I have a problem. In his defense, we were in college, and most college relationships I was exposed to were similar to my own. But that doesn't mean it was healthy. I white-washed the red flags I saw and focused long and hard on all his redeeming qualities. He had similar passions and interests. He was incredibly sweet, athletic, and attractive. He liked me for me. And best of all, he was from the East Coast (East Coast men have a certain *je ne sais quoi* in my opinion).

Throwing all logic out the door, I stayed. In fact, I conformed. As I've matured, I've had less and less of a desire to heavily drink because, as an athlete, it inhibits my performance at the gym, not to mention the gnarly hangovers I've experienced far too many times. But there I was, throwing back shots and drinking until I blacked out, pretending I liked it just so he would accept me.

I also ignored him like he ignored me from time to time. He didn't talk to me at all for a week? That's cool. Two can play that game. But deep down, I hated myself for becoming something I absolutely was not. I was toxic to both myself and my relationship. I can't blame him for the end of our relationship when I played my part as well.

When opening up to Nadine about my past, she had a similar story to tell. Like with many toxic relationships, Nadine mentioned she was not in the right headspace during the start and duration of their relationship. Because she was not healthy mentally and emotionally, she ignored many of the red flags from the start. For example, he still had dating apps downloaded on his phone throughout the duration of the relationship, lacked respect for women, lacked intentionality in the relationship, and gaslit her about his behavior in the relationship.

SO WHO & WHAT IS A NARCISSIST?

If those red flags weren't bad enough, Nadine's ex portrayed many narcissistic tendencies. Growing up, I thought narcissistic people were simply vain. I thought they were the kind of people who sat around all day thinking they're the center of the world, that they were the prettiest, that they were the best of the best. While that might be partially true, Adriana Bucci, a narcissistic abuse life coach, explained the behaviors and attitudes of a true narcissist.

As I sat down to talk to Adriana, she explained how, "in a nutshell, they need to get some form of supply from you. And that's usually your emotional reaction and that gives them some sort of sick sense of joy. . . . That is basically how you would know that somebody is a narcissist" (Bucci, 27.00).

Narcissism is manipulative, toxic, and unfortunately prevalent. Adriana explained how too often, people enter narcissistic relationships because they simply do not know better. They don't know their partner is abusive; instead, they simply think this behavior is "normal" or should just be put up with. They don't know what the red flags are, so they continue in these relationships with theoretical blindfolds on.

According to Adriana, these red flags start off with love bombing, which is showering another with "I love you's" and verbal affirmations right off the bat. Some examples are "I've never met anybody like you before," or, "You're the best person I've ever met in my life." It's all "too fast, too soon, and too flattery." Then, once you reach the same level of interest as the other, the narcissist begins to devalue you. In other words, that's when the slight little digs will come out, and that's when you discover you no longer share the thing or interest you thought you both had in common. They will gaslight you and deny anything they originally said. They will say you are overreacting or being too sensitive (Bucci, 30.00).

For a familial relationship with either a mother or father, this will look a little different. Adriana said "a lot of the time with narcissistic mothers or fathers, they can just be very controlling. And they don't let you be yourself, they don't allow you to be a human, and they force you to be responsible for their emotions.... They do the gaslighting to where they make you question your reality" (Bucci, 31.00).

THE POWER OF EMOTIONS

Regardless of the kind of toxic or narcissistic relationship you might find yourself in, all these behaviors do one thing to a person: they break you down mentally, emotionally, and physically. As Adriana told me her own story of abuse, she talked about the mind-body connection, which in short says both your mind and physical body are intertwined.

Growing up, Adriana's mother was a narcissist, but she did not think much of it at first. In her adult life, she began to experience extreme amounts of jaw pain after having her wisdom teeth removed. Adriana tried everything to get her pain under control.

As if her pain couldn't get worse, Adriana developed trigeminal neuralgia, which affects "the nerve on the side of your face that branches off into three spots." When this nerve is inflamed for whatever reason, the pain becomes absolutely unbearable. Trigeminal neuralgia has since been named the "suicide disease" because of the immense amount of pain people experience (Bucci, 15.00).

From numbing injections on the sides of her face to Botox, nothing seemed to work. It's safe to say, Adriana had hit rock bottom. But while amid this pain crisis, Adriana came across the idea of the mind-body connection, a concept rooted in the idea that your mental and emotional health impact your physical health.

She diligently began "doing the inner work," something she had neglected to do for so, so long. Within two weeks, Adriana began to feel the effects of this inner emotional work and can now say she no longer deals with chronic pain.

Often, I don't think we understand just how important our emotional states are. We often brush off our feelings and neglect to deal with the hard stuff because, well, it's hard. No one wants to sit down and talk about this trauma or that trauma. But it's vital, not only for our future relationships, but for our wellbeing. If we disregard our emotional and mental health, our emotional pain can manifest in our bodies, leaving us incapacitated.

We unknowingly allow our unresolved emotional pain to subconsciously run our lives. From entering one toxic relationship after the other, to constantly feeling exhausted, depressed, or anxious, these patterns and feelings eventually make you hit a wall. If you don't start paying attention to the signs, you'll keep repeating these cycles until you are left feeling helpless, desperate, and in pain.

STOPPING THE TANGO ONCE & FOR ALL

So how exactly do you break these toxic cycles? Well, it takes work, and a lot of it. But it's worth it. Adriana says the first step is to address and feel those emotions you have bottled up. If we don't fully feel, accept, and come to terms with our emotional state, these emotions are then stored in our bodies. To release them, you must "literally let yourself feel." Oftentimes, this involves triggering yourself to a certain extent. "Triggering yourself" isn't out of malicious intent or doesn't have to be extremely jarring. Simply recalling those memories in a safe place will allow you to begin to acknowledge the past pain and trauma. Once you begin to acknowledge and begin to experience these past emotions, journaling about how you feel, talking it out with a licensed therapist or friend, praying to God, or doing some sort of shadow work mediation are some perfect ways to address these unresolved feelings. Adriana says the best thing to do is to honor the fact that the emotions are there (Bucci, 40.00).

"Let yourself feel it. It's going to feel intense because they're very intense emotions... and when you do feel that intensity, just notice where it is in your body. Just tune into that body part and see if it moves around because emotions are a very physical process" (Bucci, 24.30).

Because our emotional health is tied in with our physical health, our emotions can be a very visceral experience. That's okay! Eventually, the emotions will reach maximum intensity and will begin to die down. As they die down, that's when the emotions are being released from your body. It's also important to note that when you allow yourself to feel these types of deep emotions, it's important you are in a safe environment. Don't try this on your commute to work or right before you're about to go to a party. Do this on a day off or when you have ample time to reflect on your experience and what you are truly feeling (Bucci, 24.30).

Becoming aware of past traumas and working through the nitty-gritty of those emotions can feel taxing and deflating. It can feel as if you are taking a few steps back. I recently heard a quote: you have to be willing to take a few steps back to be launched forward. It's easy to look around at your family or friends and compare yourself. They do not struggle like you do. They don't feel emotions in such an intense way. But they are also not you. Chances are, they probably have not taken the time yet to reflect on past traumas that are subconsciously affecting them still to this day—because most people haven't. Most people go around on autopilot. They go wherever the wind takes them, and they don't have much direction in terms of their emotional or mental health. So, while this process of reflection can feel as if you are backtracking, in reality, you are setting yourself up to be propelled ahead of the pack.

For me personally, this process has taken a very long time. I'm realizing the act of acknowledging my own pain is not isolated to one specific moment in time but takes a lifetime of continual acknowledgment and reflection. It's this act of continual acknowledgment that heals us from destructive behaviors.

For Nadine, "It is important to make sure that you are both on the same page." Whether you are "dating with the intention to marry" or in a platonic relationship, "living a life with intention" is important. By incorporating intentionality into a relationship, especially in a romantic relationship, it allows both parties to walk through the relationship with peace of mind and respect for each other. When that is not present, it can be difficult to sustain the relationship during a difficult season.

Going back to boundaries, Nadine and I have had a million and one conversations about the importance of and struggle with setting boundaries in the various relationships in our lives. Setting boundaries from the get-go is an ideal and intentional way to set up a relationship for success. Whether it be a platonic or romantic relationship, knowing your emotional, mental, and physical boundaries and communicating them effectively and openly will help your relationships thrive, rather than struggle under the weight of any unnecessary pressure.

At the end of the day, you oversee yourself. You oversee who you link arms with. You oversee how you communicate your boundaries and expectations. You oversee your healing.

This healing is vital because once it begins, you then can work through toxic patterns and recognize these traits in yourself and others. This is how to break free from the toxicity in your life. It's not by willing yourself out of it. Rather, it's by the simple acknowledgment and recognition of our past experiences and the behaviors around us that will allow you to walk into healthy, happier, and more freeing relationships with one another.

CHAPTER SIX

#METOO

Remember learning about sex in school? The teacher would be standing at the front of the classroom. A bunch of pubescent-aged kids would be awkwardly squirming in their seats as the teacher began to talk about "it."

Sex.

A slight look of horror would always dance across the faces of a few, including myself. In my freshman year of high school, my sex-ed teacher showed the class pictures of genital warts, to which I swiftly and properly covered my eyes with my hands.

Who wants to see that? Especially at 9:00 a.m. on a Monday. I just ate breakfast an hour ago, and you're about to see my half-digested Cheerios on this table if you make me look one more time. But alas, my teacher called me out in front of the class and told me he would keep the picture up on the screen until I finally looked.

I let out a sigh and took my hands off my face.

If this is what sex does, I do not want any part of it! I thought to myself.

After my class had finished looking at more STI-plagued genitalia, we began to learn about partying—or more particularly, what can happen at parties. My teacher began to explain all the things that can go wrong when you have a little too much alcohol in your system. We've all heard the saying, "nothing good happens after midnight." For the most part, that seems to be relatively true.

He talked about date rape drugs and groping and having sex without consent. We proceeded to watch some old "educational" video from the 1980s about the importance of consent and what can happen if you're not careful. The moderator of the video was a man dressed in this terrible striped vest and chunky glasses. He looked like he had not showered in at least a week, and he constantly made jokes about how sex was like a delicate flower.

Again, I thought, *If this is what sex is, I do not want any part of it!*

But of course, times change—you grow up, you learn, and you become a little more *adventurous*, let's say. If there's one thing I've learned, it's that sex and sexual assault or harassment aren't really anything like we learned at school or at home (if your parents even ventured down that path). Sex is natural and not as shameful as teachers, parents, or religious systems will tell us. Sexual assault or harassment isn't always as obvious, terrifying, or jaw-dropping as they painted it to be. Sometimes, there won't always be that big, scary man who is an obvious threat. It doesn't always happen in the sketchy, dark alleyways of your city. Sometimes, at least in my own personal experience, sexual assault or harassment is subtle, with someone you thought you trusted. Oftentimes, there's a level of manipulation that makes you think you actually want what is happening to you. It can be confusing where the line actually is, so it can be harder to ask for the help you need.

I remember the first time I was sexually assaulted. It was my first year of college, I was completely sober, and the guy who I thought was *fine* wanted me to come over. Of course my naive self just *had* to see him. I needed that goodnight kiss. But the next thing I knew, I was getting a lot more than a goodnight kiss. I won't go into the details of that event, but I do remember being utterly confused. I honestly couldn't process what was happening in the moment, but after ten minutes of squirming and trying my best to leave, I finally pushed him off me and left.

I just remember lying there in my tiny dorm-room bed. I didn't sleep a single minute that night. Instead, I just cried, finally realizing what had happened.

This wasn't supposed to happen to me. I ached as I came to terms with my reality. *This only happens to other people, not to me.*

Fast forward exactly a year later, and I decided to celebrate St. Patrick's Day like any other college kid does—by going out and drinking a little too much. Unfortunately for me, I drank *a lot* too much. But from what I do remember, I met the new guy from school who I thought was cute, and we began talking. Next thing I knew, I was back at his place, where he raped me.

As it was all happening, I remember the word "rape" popping up in my mind, knowing for a fact I never intended nor wanted to sleep with him in the first place. But in all honesty, I couldn't say anything because I was too drunk. So instead, I tried to convince myself that was what I wanted, that I was fine with it. After all, this is what every college girl does time and time again. Drunken sex is the norm, right?

As much as I wish I could say my story is rare and unusual, the statistics would say otherwise. According to RAINN, the nation's largest anti-sexual violence organization, "26.4 percent of females and 6.8 percent of males experience rape or sexual assault through physical force, violence, or incapacitation" during their undergraduate experience. For people in the LGBTQIA+ community, 23.1 percent of transgender, genderqueer, and nonconforming students have been sexually assaulted while in college ("Campus Sexual Violence").

Outside of the college atmosphere, one in every six women are victims of rape in the United States (RAINN, "Scope of the Problem"). So even though we know sexual assault and harassment is "normal"—as disgusting as that is to say—we don't normalize it in daily conversations. Rather than have open conversations and share our vulnerable stories, we shove it up on the top shelf, never to be touched or seen. I get it, though, it's scary to open up about these issues because we think we won't be believed or understood, or we will be seen as something broken and unfixable. I was sexually assaulted six times while in college, and sharing my story is something that terrifies me because I'm afraid that people from my past will come back to tell me I am wrong or untruthful.

I'm afraid of how my family will perceive me; growing up in a very conservative household, sex and sexual assault were rarely talked about and were considered taboo subjects. I've been afraid to bring it up to my friends because I have never wanted to bring the mood down. I don't think people will ever understand just how much this has deeply affected me. It's something I think about every day. It's the reason why I am afraid of most men and push guys away so readily. It's one of the most heartbreaking and painful things that has ever happened to me, and I've never wanted to be confused as weak for feeling this way. But I know I need to talk about it because if I don't, this cycle of silencing victims will continue.

THE FIGHT AGAINST SEXUAL HARASSMENT & OTHER FORMS OF GENDER-BASED VIOLENCE

But while sexual assault is unfortunately common, it is not the only form of gender-based violence. Other forms can be even more subtle and insidious, but just as harmful. Thankfully, there are women like Gina Martin, a women's and minority gender advocate who is doing her part to stop sexual harassment in its tracks by spearheading the UK's policies around this issue.

Standing there in her vibrant, red power suit, Gina Martin meant business. Cool, calm, and collected, Gina captivated the audience with her fiery eyes, gleaming with an anger that bubbled from within in a packed auditorium in Warwick, England.

"Anger is a very normal response to having our human rights compromised," she exclaimed as her voice became stern (Martin, 2020). She commanded the room.

Back in 2017, Gina and her sister attended a summertime festival in Hyde Park. What should've been a day full of cheerful memories for the twenty-somethings became the catalyst for epic change for women and marginalized genders in England. While waiting for The Killers to begin their set, Gina and her sister were near a group of guys.

"One of the guys was making loads of gross jokes and generally being really weird and harassing us. We asked him to leave us alone multiple times, but he wouldn't," Gina explained.

After telling the men to stop, Gina thought her harassment was over. But a few minutes later, more laughing came from the men. She knew it was about her. Curious and determined to find out the reason for their hysteria, Gina peered behind one of the guys to find him looking at a photo of a female—to put plainly—crotch. One of the boys had peered under a woman's skirt while at the concert and taken the picture to show his friends. Gina instantly knew it was her.

As rage boiled up inside of her, Gina yelled at him about what he had done. Disgusted with his actions and feeling violated, Gina took his phone as a crowd began to surround her. With the help of a few people, she was able to escape the scene. She ran. Weaving in and out of the crowd, the boy pursued her, desperate to retrieve what he believed was stolen.

Finding safety with the security guard, Gina got the police involved. Yet, to her utter dismay, the police acted dismissive and useless. Gina's case was dropped for two reasons: 1) the photo was not graphic enough, and 2) there was no law protecting people from "upskirting."

"Something inside me sort of snapped. I had been dealing with sexual harassment for as long as I could remember, and I've been brushing it off. I was so over it. I couldn't believe there wasn't a law covering it in some way, so I started to try to look into it, and everything I read was written by politicians and lawmakers and academic people who spoke with jargon. They don't speak like me."

Gina notes there are two options when one experiences sexual harassment or assault: 1) you brush it off and shut up, or 2) you do something about it, no matter how small the action is. Because these laws and policies are often complex and confusing, women and marginalized genders often remain silent, unable to speak out themselves. With the complexity of the law and societal conditioning, those marginalized have been groomed to suppress their voices.

"Number one I think has affected me more than I know. Because of number one, when I watch news stories about this stuff, I start crying out of nowhere. When someone tells me a story about sexual harassment, it somehow partly feels like it's done [to me] because of number one. Because of number one, I have struggled to articulate this problem for such a long time because I shut my mouth about it and I didn't have the language. I'm frustrated that year after year, number one seems like our best option."

While the option to shut up and be silent seems to be the safer option for many, the option to speak out and do something is something that must be done—for there is power behind action. Finally standing up for herself, Gina posted a photo of herself at the festival with her antagonist in the background. In hopes of finding out who her perpetrator was, Gina asked people on Facebook to identify the man. But Gina's request was quickly shot down. According to Facebook, her actions constituted as harassment.

Angry and frustrated, Gina needed a new plan of attack. She was willing to do anything to reclaim a sense of what she had lost—her dignity.

"We have to stop using [anger] to delegitimize people with 'angry feminist' or 'angry Black woman.' People are allowed to be angry about this stuff, and we have to hold space for them there. You have to realize it's not about us."

She is right; it's not about us. This fight against sexism is not about who is right or wrong. It's not about pointing fingers. It's something much bigger than Gina or anyone else could imagine. It's about justice and equality. It's about holding people accountable for invisible and disrespectful actions. It's about becoming a society that puts integrity and the wellbeing of others at the forefront.

Fueled by her anger, sadness, and disbelief, Gina did what she knew how to do best: she started a social media and political campaign fighting against sexism in society.

"Social media is the single most democratizing tool we've ever had for social change. It can be harnessed for good at any time, by anyone. Traditional institutions don't yet understand it properly. Use that."

As the campaign gained steam, Gina's DMs flooded with heartbreaking stories of women and children affected by the humiliating nature of upskirting. As the messages came in, one group of messages, in particular, seemed to haunt Gina to the very core. Several children from a school in South London reached out to Gina about a teacher who had been known to upskirt the young girls. Come to find out, the teacher had been collecting thousands of graphic photos of his students for months (Martin, 2020).

The only problem? There was still no law protecting from upskirting.

Finally, with the help of a lawyer, Gina helped to create new legislation protecting women and marginalized genders from the act of upskirting. The proposed law stated any individual on summary conviction can be imprisoned for up to twelve months if he or she upskirted someone without consent (UK Public General Acts, 2019). After one year of meeting after meeting, the new legislation was passed in January 2019, in its entirety, with no additional amendments to the originally proposed bill.

Within its first year of its passing, the new bill helped to prosecute ten men, all of these being pedophiles or sexual predators.

"All misogyny and sexual violence are connected. Therefore, all of it is the problem. None of it is trivial. We have to remember that," Gina proclaimed as her speech came to a close. "There will be one phrase that comes up again and again. It's not the scariest I've dealt with, but it is the most effective at derailing this important conversation . . . It will say: not all men. To that, I'll say this: no, not all men, but too many. Too many men, for some reason, feel entitled to women and marginalized gender bodies. Too many men, whether through action or inaction, are perpetuating a culture of sexism that breeds inequality, and that leads to violence" (Martin, 2020).

WHY YOU SHOULD CARE

While rape, sexual assault, and sexual harassment happen to people of all different genders, women and other minority genders are most affected. Like mentioned before, one out of every six women will experience rape in her lifetime, yet only one out of every thirty-three men will experience rape in his lifetime (RAINN, "Scope of the Problem"). Out of every ten rape victims, nine of them will have been women. Like Gina states, all misogyny and sexual violence is connected. According to Stop Street Harassment—a nonprofit "dedicated to documenting and ending gender-based street harassment worldwide"—76 percent of women and 35 percent of men in the US have experienced verbal sexual harassment. On a more global level, more than 90 percent of women claim to have experienced some form of public harassment during their lifetime (Kearl, 2011).

Many would say Gina's views are quite stark and dramatic, but she has a point. Compared to men, this issue is affecting women and minority genders drastically more. In today's society and culture, it can be so easy to tell a woman to put on more clothes or stop "asking" for it—a phrase used too often. But based on these statistics, if almost all women in their lifetimes are experiencing harassment to a greater or lesser degree, shouldn't we be questioning our own logic? Is it really the women who need to stop acting and dressing in a certain way? Or is this more men's issue?

In her final conclusion, Gina reminds us that oppressed communities should not be left alone to dismantle what has been built against them. Rather, others must use their privilege to assist. As for men, they are the ones who have the most privilege of all. They are called to do their part: to educate themselves, to listen to others, and to change their actions. Dismantling the patriarchal system set in place is not an easy road to tread, and the chances of sexual violence being completely demolished in our lifetime are slim to none. It's just the bitter truth of it all. But it doesn't mean we shouldn't try—especially men.

Now, I am not saying women have no power in changing the current system without the help of men. As women, we are incredibly resourceful in finding other ways to advocate for ourselves and for our young girls. The #MeToo movement, for example, has been a pivotal movement in the fight against sexual violence against women and minority genders. By using social media, publicly advocating for ourselves has been easier than ever before. However, we still need men to do their part because, without them, these laws and behaviors have a higher likelihood of leaving women and marginalized groups disoriented, confused, frustrated, and silenced. We need men to fight this fight against sexual violence because, if they don't, women and other minority genders have a higher chance of remaining disempowered and vulnerable. We need men to do their part because, if they don't, women might never have the possibility of stepping out into who they were meant to be.

CHAPTER SEVEN

SEXY & I OWN IT!

Imagine: A room full of middle school girls gathered in an auditorium, waiting in anticipation for the talent show finale to start. The talent show finale *never* disappointed, and this year would be no different.

The stage suddenly went dark, and moments later a single beam of light shined from above. Then, swiftly, a line of eighth-grade boys scurries out. The boys just so happened to have gone to PE right before the big finale, so there was a certain *je ne said quoi* in the air. But that didn't matter to the eager seventh-grade girls. The eighth-grade boys were *hot*, dare we say sexy?

Seconds later, the lights came on. The boys started to awkwardly dance, throwing in hip thrusts and other sexually suggestive dance moves. The girls went crazy. It was madness. To really amplify these eighth-grade boys' *sexy masculinity*, they danced to "Sexy and I Know It" by LMFAO. It was truly an iconic moment.

I hate to admit it, but I was one of those seventh-grade girls in the auditorium that day. I can remember it like it was yesterday. My middle school crush looked so good up there as he sexually danced and gyrated up on stage. He was the definition of sexy at the time, or at least I thought so.

But as the years have gone by, I often look back at that moment and think: Why? Why did every middle school girl that day think being sexy and sexual were synonymous? As if you can't have one without the other?

Growing up, there was one word I had best not utter unless I wanted an entire lecture on it, which was *sex*.

Honestly, nothing disgusted me more than my parents talking to me about this "act" because it made me want to vomit. Each time my parents tried to make me watch some vastly outdated sexual education videos from the '80s that they got from my school counselor, I threw a fit. It was pure torture. I had so many questions like: 1) why was everything about this topic so freaking awkward, 2) and why was there this "hush-hush" nature surrounding this topic? After all, if this was so natural, then why weren't we talking about it like it was?

The years went on, and I obviously have gotten more comfortable with the topic—even if the mechanics of it all remain slightly strange if you think about it long enough. But regardless of it all, sex and sexuality—particularly female sexuality—have always intrigued me. Everyone seems to have either an incredibly harsh and blunt opinion regarding the matter or no opinion at all. As someone who often has strong opinions and views on various topics, I have to be honest and say I am still figuring out what I think of it all.

It's safe to say we live in a highly sexualized society. From Carl's Jr. television commercials to provocative billboard ads, females especially have been painted as these sexy, provocative, and sultry babes for the sake of marketing. When I was around the age of eight years old, I would spend hours on end flipping through *TigerBeat* and *J-14 Magazine*, both predominant teen magazines at the time, and would see images upon images of stick-thin actresses and models wearing little to nothing when at the grocery store and the red carpet. These teen celebrities were publicized as sexual beings when, in reality, many were still minors.

In kindergarten, I remember showing up to school in my typical outfit: a cute floral dress with my hair a mess. It was lunchtime, and my little, chubby legs took me to the playground. I couldn't find any of my friends, so I decided to head back to the classroom to find some people to play with. I was happy to see a group of my friends sitting at the lunch tables and decided to join them. But right as I made my way over to the table, the entire group of girls stood up to face me. As we began to talk, I noticed each one of the girls were wearing platform sandals, a crop top, a jean skirt, and little hoop earrings. Essentially, my friends looked like they were five going on sixteen. They told me their outfits were something Britney Spears would wear, and if I wasn't going to dress like them, then I couldn't play with them that day. Then, with a swing in their hips, they all walked away, leaving me in the dust.

I went home that day and asked my mom if I could dress like they did so I could be accepted, and she answered with a stern "*No!*"

"It's not appropriate for girls your age to be wearing things like that," my mom told me. "You'd be asking for it."

I was five years old, and I didn't know what "asking for it" really meant, but I decided to trust her and just nodded my head in slight disappointment. But as I grew up, I couldn't help but notice how women of all ages were portrayed in the media. They were all skinny, sexy, and popular, and this seemed like the trifecta I needed to be a part of.

So, I would give my subpar attempt at doing what you needed to do to be "accepted." I followed all the fashion trends, I bought way too many clothes from Justice (does anyone remember those sparkly monkey shirts?), and I tried to stay up to date with all the hairstyle trends that my favorite celebrities, like Hilary Duff and Miley Cyrus, rocked. But because of my parents' conservative household and my lack of true interest in anything "girly," I was never able to achieve this sexy, popular look I tried so hard to get. I never wore makeup until college. I wore skinny jeans and clunky tennis shoes until someone in middle school told me that was not a "cute" look. I think shopping is time-consuming and boring. Because of all these factors, I told myself I was more on par with the tomboys than I was with the girly girls.

It wasn't until about my senior year of high school, I think, that I started to come into my own, develop my own sense of style, and become more comfortable in my skin. As college rolled around and I started to make friends, I noticed boys were actually paying attention to me for the first time ever. I'm not going to lie, I loved it! As someone who has felt somewhat invisible in the past, this sudden interest from men really lit me up. But there was one issue: I didn't know how to play the part of this "cute, sexy blonde girl."

So, like any Gen Z gal, I took to social media to find inspiration, validation, or a mixture of both for my new identity I wanted to create. I started wearing lots of crop tops and more revealing clothes because Brandy Melville had just hit the fashion scene and anyone who was anyone wore them. I started wearing makeup, not much I'll admit, but more than I ever had before. I blow-dried my hair every day because having heat-damaged hair was all the rage, or so I heard.

To be completely honest, I really did like my new look. I could finally wear things that both my mom and dad would probably have fallen out of their chairs over if they saw me wearing them, but I was a free woman and that meant wearing what was "in." More and more guys would come up to me, ask me out, and ask me to their dances. I was truly flattered, but now there was a new issue I was facing: I didn't know how to keep up this "cute, sexy blonde girl" act. It was exhausting. The constant upkeep of my appearance took too long. Always having to look cute, always having to feel pretty, always slapping a smile on my face even when my shorts wouldn't stop riding up my butt that day was ridiculous. The whole thing started to feel like a show.

Chances are, I'm not alone in feeling this way. The media portrayed women as being sexual beings long before social media and television came to be, but the use of mass advertisements and the introduction of the iPhone has created an era where any source of news, advertisement, or marketing can reach us in the blink of an eye. Megan Maas said there's a difference between being sexual versus acting sexual, and in our current climate, we get those two confused far too often.

"Deborah Toleman—she's an expert in female adolescent sexual development—talks about acting sexual versus being sexual," Maas said. "Acting sexual is kind of like a performance, meaning you are really focused, like, on your lingerie and your makeup and how you look. You're going to make sure you do these certain [sex] positions because you know your boobs look great in that position and they don't look great in this position." These are examples of performing sexuality.

On the contrary, being sexual "has to do with really noticing what your body's experiencing in the moment, what kinds of sensations feel good, and what kinds of [emotional] connection feel good." According to Maas, men seem to have an easier time being sexual than women. For women, being sexual is a lot harder due to our sexual socialization. Sexual socialization is "a multidimensional process by which knowledge, attitudes, and values about sexuality are acquired" (*Encyclopedia of Sexuality and Gender, 2021*). The media obviously has a lot to do with how we see and think about things. The male gaze, for example, has been portrayed in film since Hollywood began in its glory days. This gaze "suggests a sexualized way of looking that empowers men and objectifies women" (Loreck, 2016). As women, we've all felt it at least once. That random guy on the bus staring at you for too long, or the guy at the coffee shop who just can't seem to take his eyes off you. This male gaze can feel all-encompassing at times, yet women often fall prey to it. Often, women don't dress sexy for themselves, but rather for the approval of men. Women have allowed this sexual socialization to influence them in ways many are not consciously aware of.

With social media, and particularly apps like Instagram, experts say its impact is far greater than we ever realized. According to a study done by Stefanie E. Davis back in 2018, the "use of image-based social media platforms like Instagram is linked to greater self-objectification." Many people often use Instagram to "observe and monitor attractive peers," and "combined with exposure to increasingly sexualized mass media," which stimulates self-objectification and critical self-surveillance over time (Davis, 2018). It's easy to see the sexualization of the female body anywhere. All you have to do is pick up your phone, turn on the TV, or drive past a billboard. With this increase of female sexuality portrayed in the media, self-objectification and self-surveillance have been linked to the misunderstanding or misrepresentation of peer norms regarding sex.

I honestly couldn't imagine being a pre-teen or teenager in today's day and age. I was greatly influenced by those now outdated teen magazines. But now, pre-teens and teenagers are bombarded with exaggerated visuals of women and their bodies via social media. Every day, pre-teens and teens on social media get messages implying how they are supposed to act and dress just to fit in. If I were a teen now, I would be left in a puddle of confusion.

How should I act? What should I wear? How should I see myself? These are the questions I would have no answer to.

As you grow older and become more in tune with your sexuality, your questions can become more amplified and intense. Like, what do I have to do to get this person to like me? Do I have to sleep with them even if I don't feel comfortable with them? Why does the idea of sex and my sexual being make me so uncomfortable?

Growing up in a culture that deems sex and sexuality as a fairly taboo topic, young women can be incredibly confused about their thoughts and be quick to believe any information they see online or hear from family and friends. According to Maas, only eleven states in the US are required to have medically accurate sex education. That means the sex educators in the thirty-nine other states in the US can give false information to their students. No wonder there seems to be so many conflicting views on sex! Few and far between are properly educated!

With this confusion of sex and sexuality, many people are taking to pornography to "learn" what sex really is. The problem? Porn portrays a hyper-sexualized, unrealistic view of sex. Oftentimes, porn portrays a dismissive, patriarchal attitude toward women and children. Maas mentioned that with the ubiquity of porn, people not only have "access to [other] people having sex but access to crazy kinds of sex." Because of these false narratives of what and how a sexual encounter can look like, "people tend to have unrealistic expectations about what a sexual interaction is going to look like, and there's more pressure to behave a certain way."

You don't have to actively watch porn to be affected by these skewed narratives of sex. Pornographic images are prevalent and widely accessible on social media sites and find their way into the everyday advertisements we see. The bombardment of these sexy, provocative images has undeniable effects on women. In a study titled "Objectification, Sexualization, and Misrepresentation: Social Media and the College Experience," researchers looked at the portrayal of both male and female sexuality on Instagram accounts such as College Nationwide and Four Year Party. From their findings, they found an overwhelming portrayal of female objectification, women as submissive creatures, and the emphasis of the young, white college experience.

On many of these types of college party-related Instagram accounts, you can find nameless young women in no clothing with their back to the camera. Many of these women are shaking their boobs and ass, and are pretty, young, and predominantly white. Scroll through any of these accounts, and this is what you will find. By no means am I slut-shaming these women. I did the booty-shaking contest in Cabo (I got second place). But when we post things like this on social media for the whole world to see, rather than just the fifty people at that party, we're inviting a whole host of opinions, comments, and eyes into the mix. By portraying women in this light, it's easy to purely sexualize a woman when she remains merely boobs and a hot body. From how she thinks of herself to how she copes with her mental and emotional health, women and young girls can face intense effects from this social sexualization. Studies show mental health, self-esteem, eating disorders, and a whole array of negative emotional side effects are linked to this sexualization of women (Sheppard, 2020).

These socially constructed views of sexuality easily translate into our ideas and opinions of sex. Obviously, everyone has his or her own personal views on sex depending on how he or she was raised, what culture he or she grew up in, and what religious or spiritual denomination he or she identifies with. But regardless of those factors, the current social culture surrounding sex and sexuality plays a huge role in how society views the topic as a whole.

I personally think one of the main issues we have in America is we often separate our sexual self from the rest of our identity. Megan Maas said one's sexual self "should be intertwined with who you are, but usually Americans tend to compartmentalize our sexuality." So instead, we refrain from talking about it, and we act like it's this thing that happens "that we're so driven by, but yet we're not in control of."

What if Americans stopped being so afraid of our sexual selves? I don't mean we have to go around sleeping with anyone and everyone. Quite the opposite. We have developed this mentality around sex and sexuality that it is purely for show, that if you sleep with so many people you are considered either legendary or a whore with no in-between. Often, this is gendered. Women are disproportionally slut-shamed for having a lot of sex with different people compared to men. In addition, we have become so focused on these sexual "conquests"—both men and women—that we have lost sight of why we do these things. For women, sex is what both cool girls and sluts do—a dichotomy women will never be able to live up to. This idea often plays into the "girl next door" trope. As women, we are supposed to be sexy and desirable, but innocent and unaware of it.

Regardless of whether you choose to save yourself for marriage or not, I think it's important to understand you are a sexual being, just like you are an emotional, physical, mental, and spiritual being. To be a sexual being doesn't mean you have to engage in sexual acts you don't want. It doesn't mean you have to put on this performance where you wear some incredibly uncomfortable lingerie that rides up your butt just so your man will like it. It doesn't mean you have this incapability of controlling your sex drive; you do, it just comes down to whether you want to or not.

To me, being sexy and embracing your sexual self is being comfortable in your own skin. It means owning your body as you are and not trying to look like a model *People Magazine* tells you to be. It means getting up on stage in a country bar and shaking it—not for the attention of others, but because you're just looking to have a fun and memorable night with your girlfriends. It means wearing a cute pair of Lululemon leggings because I feel conformable in them and my butt looks nice—a double whammy! To be sexy is to be comfortable in your own skin and celebrate the body God gave you.

I think it's perfectly fine to be a "sexy" person. When I ask my friends, they will always describe me as having a "sexy" style, and I do! I'm the girl who's worn crop tops and miniskirts to church before without any shame! (God thought I looked great). While I probably wouldn't wear the same things as I did a few years ago, I still wear clothes that make me feel confident and sexy in my own way. The point is, I'm not wearing clothes that will gain approval from any outside source. I dress and act according to how I feel. If I want to dress a little sexy one night because I'm feeling it, I do it! But if it's a leggings or sweatpants kind of day, I'll wear that and still feel like my confident and sexy self. I think, as women, we need to begin to redefine our own definition of what it means to be sexual. We too often let society and culture dictate our definition of sex and sexuality, and it leaves us confused about our own sex life and sexuality. It's important to determine your own beliefs and thoughts on the matter, and everyone's opinions, thought, and beliefs regarding sex and sexuality are going to look different, which is okay. Frankly, I think your personal sexual boundaries are between you and God alone. But we need to start redefining these narratives around what it means to be sexy and how female sexuality looks like, because if we don't, culture will continue to do so for us. This hyper-sexual culture we live in is toxic and leaves many feeling victimized, exploited, and full of shame.

Sexy can be subtle and shameless. I think we all need to remember that.

CHAPTER EIGHT

FAITH, SHAME & THE PATRIARCHY

I was raised in an incredibly religious, Protestant household and community where a strong faith in God is adored and celebrated. I went to a strict Christian school until the seventh grade, went to church almost every Sunday, and was taught to give my worries to the good Lord. At school, I was told to never touch alcohol before the age of twenty-one and to never even think about having sex before marriage. For the longest time, God and religion seemed like this big omniscient ghost ready to crack down their golden hammer any time. While God (and religion) seemed like this big, ominous being, I was never really terrified of Him . . . until one day in my therapist's office.

I was eighteen years old and about to graduate high school. I was nervous, wringing my hands wildly in my lap, my heart racing.

"Okay, so. Um . . ." I simply couldn't say it. I didn't want to admit it, but I decided to swallow my pride. *Here goes nothing*, I thought.

"I drank last night," I blurted out. "Like, only three drinks. I didn't get too drunk. But I drank, and I feel so much shame. Like, I feel like God is mad at me, and my parents would absolutely kill me!"

Oh sweet, sweet Sarah, if only you knew half of the things you would do later in life, you wouldn't feel ashamed.

My therapist sat there looking at me. It was the kind of look you get from someone right before they laugh at how pathetic you are. But she didn't laugh. Instead, she just sat there nodding her head.

Eventually, she went on to say something insignificant I can no longer recall. All I do remember was she was utterly useless when attending to my situation. I left her office that day thinking and praying. I prayed God would take the shame away. I prayed I could be the perfect Christian girl I thought He and my parents wanted me to be. I prayed I could live a life without being haunted by every wrong decision.

While my story might seem personal, isolated, and slightly dramatic, I know many people share a similar story to me.

According to the 2014 US Religious Landscape Study, 70.6 percent of Americans identify as Christian, with varying denominations. While many people are not practicing Christians, many Christian doctrines and principles are the foundation of our country's constitution, culture, and way of thinking. A great example of Christian religious beliefs influencing our government's policies is the debate of *Roe v. Wade*.

ROE V. WADE

On January 22, 1973, the US Supreme Court legalized abortion across the United States. *Roe v. Wade* is deemed as one of the most controversial cases in American history, as it deals with terminating premature fetuses ("Roe v. Wade," 2019). To many Protestants and Catholics, life is a gift from God and starts from the moment of conception, therefore, according to many Christians (but not all), having an abortion is murder. Pro-life advocates often use their religious beliefs to influence their way of voting, rather than set aside their religious views when doing so. Many view this issue as either right or wrong, black or white. In all actuality, this human rights issue has no easy solution, but is multifaceted and technicolored.

Roe v. Wade is also seen as a right to privacy issue according to the Fourteenth Amendment. Many women worry that if this is ever overturned, there could be a domino effect relating to the overturn of women's privacy rights, such as access to birth control and access to Planned Parenthood. *Roe v. Wade* is one of the most legendary Supreme Court cases, especially relating to women's overall rights and equality. Though this case specifically related to women, the original, deciding jury in 1973 was all men (Filipovic, 2018). Any red flags raised? There should be.

Personally, I find *Roe v. Wade* an excellent example of the intersection of religion and patriarchy for multiple reasons. First of all, the fact that men were the sole deciding factor for a women's rights issue is alarming. While the verdict did improve the reproductive rights of women, it very well could have gone the other way. In addition, many of the opponents of *Roe v. Wade* are religious groups, as I mentioned previously. In many ancient holy texts (including but not exclusive to the Bible), female sexuality is portrayed as something that should be hidden rather than celebrated. Consequently, much of that toxic ideology has infiltrated conservative religious views. This mesh of patriarchy, the lack of separation between the church and state, and the shaming of women is unsettling and detrimental to women's overall freedoms.

While I am pro-choice, I also want to acknowledge the fact that this topic is very unsettling and triggering for some, and I know I will offend others. But, staying on trend with my writing, I think it is imperative I capture and voice my current thoughts and feelings regarding topics I am passionate about, yet often shy away from. As a twenty-three-year-old Christian woman, I still question what is right and what is wrong when it comes to this topic, but at the end of the day, I know I could never walk in another's shoes. Therefore, while I might not make such a decision, I find supporting and honoring women through their own personal journeys without perpetuating guilt or shame is the most loving decision I can personally make.

WHY ARE ALL THE MEN AT THE PULPITS?

Unfortunately, *Roe v. Wade* is just one example of the intersection of religion and patriarchy. Many leaders of the Christian and Catholic Churches are prime examples of misogyny at play. Let me start with this question: Have you ever attended, or at least seen a depiction, of a predominantly female clergy? Back in 1960, it was estimated that around 2 percent of women held a clergy title. In the past forty years, women now represent about 20 percent of the clergy as of 2017 (Smith, 2018). However, the disparity of women in this field still provides a stark contrast to its counterpart.

So why is it that there are far more male priests and pastors than there are women? Throughout much of the Old and New Testaments in the Bible, men were revered as the heads of the household and sole leaders of society. While these books were written thousands of years ago under incredibly patriarchal societies, many of these ideologies regarding women holding power in religious settings still exists. For example, in the Roman Catholic Church, Southern Baptist Convention, Latter Day Saints, and Orthodox Church of America, it is still not supported for women to be ordained or lead a congregation (Pew Research Center, 2014).

So, it makes me wonder, what narrative are we telling women of all ages about their role in the church or other religious settings? What narratives are these women getting from the men at the pulpits every Sunday? Men, particularly white males, are considerably more privileged than women and have their own view of the world and how it works. How does this affect male interpretations of the Bible and other holy texts? I think as women, we tend to shy away from these kinds of topics because it is seen as sacrilegious to question people in holy authority. But let's flip the table for a second: Aren't women given holy authority, too?

In Proverbs 31:25–6, the author speaks of the ideal attributes of a woman, particularly the ideal attributes of a wife. It states:

> *"She is clothed with strength and dignity;*
> *she can laugh at the days to come.*
> *She speaks with wisdom,*
> *and faithful instruction is on her tongue."*

Wouldn't we showcase our wisdom if we started standing up for ourselves? Wouldn't we showcase that we have some dignity if we started pushing back and demanding equality? If "faithful instruction" is on our tongue, then why are we so afraid to lead?

It all goes back to the fact that we've been told we can't. Unfortunately, for thousands of years, people abused their power in the name of religion. As of this year, it is estimated that the Catholic Church has between $10 to $15 billion (AP, 2021). From misusing money to covering up sex scandals, the church has long exploited its monetary power for its own sake. Pope Francis said it best when he stated, "Sacramental power [has become] too closely aligned with power in general" (Dillon, 2019). Unfortunately, oftentimes these ulterior motives distort the teachings in these holy books and use shame as a tactic to control minority groups.

SHAME IS A POWERFUL WEAPON

Shame is a powerful weapon. According to the *Journal of Psychology and Theology* for Biola University, "Shame is extremely painful; it involves global negative evaluations the self. . . . Shame makes us feel condemned to our very core." Shame is the elephant in the room no one wants to talk about. Shame is the dirty little secret that hides behind the curtains, shying away from the light. Shame is an epidemic.

As a shame researcher, Brené Brown has spent much of her career discovering how shame grows and manifests in women's lives. According to her work, shame needs three things to grow: secrecy, silence, and judgment (Brown, 18:46). Unfortunately, we live in a society where behaviors like alcoholism and sexual promiscuity are shunned, silenced, and heavily judged.

Do you do drugs? Okay, keep that to yourself.

Are you struggling with living up to any societal or cultural norm? Maybe you shouldn't say anything or should just try a little harder, or else you might be seen as a failure.

With ideologies like these, we create the perfect breeding ground for shame because we never make enough room for listening, learning, and understanding. Rather, we use secrecy, silence, and judgment as the deadly antidotes to our deepest issues.

It is also important to note that shame is, in fact, gender-specific. Shame affects both men and women. However, shame is differently categorized by societal pressures and norms.

For example, women are often shamed for being busy working parents, while men are not. Women are expected to be it all: the perfect homemaker, the perfect wife, the perfect mother. We are supposed to bake and cook and clean and work. We are supposed to be soft and sweet and strong and sensitive. We are supposed to be grateful and gracious, poised and proper. To top it all off, we are supposed to be thin, but not too thin. Curvy, but not too curvy. Forever look young, but if we get plastic surgery to look younger, we just end up looking fake.

Brown stated in her famous TED Talk, "Listening to Shame": "For women, shame is do it all, do it perfectly, and never let them see you sweat. . . . Shame for women is this web of unobtainable, conflicting, competing expectations about who we're supposed to be."

This shame silently suffocates us. It grips our necks and presses on our chests. It fills our thoughts and tells us we will eventually get caught. Shame is deadly. Shame is linked to addiction, depression, violence, aggression, bullying, suicide, and eating disorders. Shame is the white underbelly of everything we shy away from.

Is there an antidote for this shame-inducing society we live in?

EMPATHY IS THE ANSWER

The answer is empathy, or more specifically, the words "me too." We all struggle from time to time. We all fail. We all cry. We all feel pain. But after our pitfalls, why do so many of us feel the need to turn around and point fingers at one another, someone who is worse off, someone who is deemed "more of a failure" than us? What happened to good old-fashioned empathy? What happened to the empathy that sits there with you at your lowest lows, at your darkest moments, during your deepest hurts?

I think oftentimes people in religious settings forget to do this exact thing. They spend so much time caught up on reforming the actions of many that they end up pushing away the exact people they want to draw near.

While it may seem as if I am bashing religion and Christianity as a whole, I am not. But I do think there needs to be a long, hard look at how people of all religious denominations deal with human shame and guilt. More specifically, I think this transformation begins on an individual level.

Personally, I have dealt with crippling shame and guilt. From drinking, partying, and sex to my own mental health and physical appearance, there have been days where the tears simply would not stop flowing. I convinced myself that God and my parents were disappointed in me.

How could you say you love Jesus, but do this sort of thing? I'd think to myself.

I'd lie there on my tiny twin bed in college and wonder if I was messing it all up. I held so many secrets in my heart for so long that I began to theoretically poison myself. The slow burn of shame haunted me day in and day out.

It wasn't until the fall of 2018 when I reached my tipping point. I was studying abroad in Italy and I was concussed, heartbroken, and the most anxious and depressed I had been since high school. I felt shame for hating my experience because I was supposed to be living "la vida dolce"—the sweet life. I thought going to Italy would be a sweet escape from my reality in San Diego, but I soon learned that problems can follow you from even ten thousand miles away.

One day while in Italy, I was on a trip to Sardinia with my best friend, also named Sarah. Based on a last-minute decision, we decided to go to the small Italian island for the weekend. It was our first solo trip, and we had absolutely no idea what we were doing. Our Airbnb host gave us some fabulous recommendations for dinner, and we began wandering the island, relying on Google Maps to show us the way. Somehow, we stumbled upon the restaurant she had suggested, which was on top of a mountain alongside an ancient castle. We got a table, drank some wine, and talked about how excited we were about both our present trip and our future. While we joked and laughed, I began to open up about the past six months of my life.

She was the first person I ever told I was raped. Rather than sit there and lecture me about how I should've reported him or ask me why I kept seeing him after the fact, she just listened. She sat there, nodding her head, leaning in, trying her best to understand. If I remember correctly, she started to cry.

I was honestly taken aback. "Why are you crying? I'm fine! I'm alive. I'm still kicking!" I said. But her tears opened a part of my heart that had been begging to be open for so, so long. I felt heard and seen. My shame left.

Sarah's empathy was the antidote to my pain and the light that flashed upon my darkness. As much as I wish I could say that moment changed everything and I went on my way living a shame-free life, I unfortunately cannot. For much of my fall semester abroad, as Sarah can attest, I was an absolute wreck, an anxious mess, and a burden to be around. Yet, she kept loving me through it all.

Sarah showed me what God's love truly means, and it was after Italy when I made a promise that I would no longer be a slave to myself. I started to learn what God's love really means. I started to really learn about the kind of person Jesus was and apply it to my own life. Fun fact, Jesus was friends with the drunkards and prostitutes, and never once made them feel ashamed of their lifestyle. Rather, He just showed them unconditional love, and they felt convicted to change their ways but did not feel condemned. In Matthew 21:31, Jesus even says, "Truly I tell you, the tax collectors and the prostitutes are entering the kingdom of God ahead of you."

At the beginning of 2020, I started to listen to pastors like Judah Smith, who is my absolute favorite. He speaks on how religion is the thing that separates us. Rather than call himself a Catholic or a Protestant, he claims to simply be a Jesus follower. In one of his most recent sermons I listened to, he said something so incredibly profound, chills ran up and down my spine: "Our life is not about rules, it's about a relationship. It's not about morals, it's about a man, and his name is Jesus. Now, instead of focusing on ten commandments, we focus on a man" (Smith, 22.00). He went on to say how today we are so focused on the destination, on what we win, and where we'll get, when we should just be focused on the walk. What if life was never about becoming someone perfect, but rather becoming someone a little better than we were the day before? What if we were never really supposed to try as hard as we do to be something that we're not?

What if your walk with God, the universe, your higher self, or whatever else you call it, was simply meant to be the journey to your most divine self?

Over these past few years, I've begun to redefine my relationship with religion. Rather than say I am religious, I would say I am a spiritual Christian. Religion is full of rules and doctrines. It's full of do's and don'ts and rights and wrongs. You must go to church. You must be a virgin. You can never drink too much, never lie, never lust, never sin. Those are impossible standards no one can meet. This, in turn, causes shame to grow.

Why not flip the narrative? Sinning is inevitable. Messing up is inevitable. Cussing is inevitable—at least for me. But luckily, for me, following Jesus is about getting better each and every day and knowing sometimes I'm going to backslide, and that's perfectly okay.

I know I focus a lot on my Christian faith in this chapter, but I want you to know regardless of what religion, spiritual practice, or lack thereof you believe in, we are all a lot closer than we think. I once took a course while in Florence about Jesus and Buddha. It turns out, Jesus and Buddha stand for many of the same principles, like love, justice, and the Golden Rule. If people stripped away the principles and thought patterns that induced shame, I think we would live in a world that was a bit kinder, nicer, and a whole lot happier.

So I'll leave with this: What do you need to bring to light that you've been hiding for so long? What's that one thing deep inside you've convinced yourself will absolutely kill you if someone knows? Have you brought it to God, the universe, or your highest self?

It's time to shed some light on your darkness, for as Dr. Martin Luther King said, "Darkness cannot drive out darkness; only light can do that."

CHAPTER NINE

THE MENTAL HEALTH PANDEMIC

Recovering from depression is like getting over a terrible hangover. At first, you think you can handle it on your own. Then, the aches and pains start to set in. The unshakable queasiness hits the pit of your stomach, and you are overcome with absolute and utter dread. You doubt yourself and realize you're in for more than you bargained for. You don't think you'll make it. It's better to stay in bed all day than face anything that requires real energy. You're helpless and feel like only half a human.

But with a whole lot of mental strength, resilience, and help from other external factors, you feed yourself, drink water, and may even gradually recover from what seems like a near-death experience. You can finally see the light at the end of the tunnel. You are safe. You can finally sigh in relief, hoping to never experience those feelings of complete anguish again.

Mental illness has the unfortunate ability to turn your life upside down and inside out. It's as if it leaves you in the middle of a drought with no access to water, completely and utterly disillusioned and desperate for a way out. It can tear you down to your core, leaving you with nothing to salvage. While mental illness is on the rise and reported more and more, especially in young teens, it still remains stigmatized and misunderstood by those who have truly never walked through it (Rosenberg, 2019).

For Sadie Sutton, depression and mental illness engulfed her every waking moment. At the start of sixth grade, Sadie noticed a change in her mindset. Her mood was often abnormally low, her sleeping and eating habits were off, and her interest in average life events hit rock bottom. Because she had begun to experience depression at such an early age, it became difficult for her to even remember a time when life wasn't depressing. Having experienced no outstanding childhood trauma, Sadie felt anger, guilt, and blame toward her parents, assuming they had caused her unhappiness. Desperate to help their daughter, Sadie's parents made her attend weekly family therapy sessions in hopes of repairing their relationship, but nothing seemed to help.

"Because I believed I didn't deserve love, every time someone would say hi to me, I'd think 'Oh, they're just saying that to me because they have to. Not because they care about me,'" Sadie explained. "I wouldn't accept any love or care people were giving me."

As her depression hit an all-time low, Sadie's relationships began to suffer even more. Her parents made the executive decision to take her to 3East at Mclean Hospital right outside of Boston. Upon arriving, Sadie was asked if she wanted to be there. To that, she answered with a strong no. Her parents were informed that if Sadie didn't want to be there, she was not expected to be.

Blaise Aguirre, MD, a top psychiatrist in the mental health field, informed Sadie that treatment "wasn't going to work unless [she] wanted to be there." In fact, he told her she wasn't "allowed to stay unless she could see the wisdom in it for herself."

Panic filled the room for a moment. Thrown into a frenzy, her parents asked the directors at Mclean Hospital, "What do you mean?" They had flown across the country to help their daughter, not to be told their daughter was helpless.

Amid the panic and chaos, Sadie began to think.

What if? What if I believed in treatment and therapy for the first time? What if I wanted to make my life something I loved? What if I really believed something could change for me, and I just went all in?

So, she agreed to stay at the hospital. Slowly but surely, Sadie began to take back control of her mental health. While at the Mclean Hospital, Sadie underwent dialectical behavioral therapy (DBT). DBT is one form of cognitive-behavioral therapy and helps patients to be present in the moment, better regulate their emotions, improve their relationships, and handle stress in healthy ways (Schimelpfening, 2021). With the help of this treatment, Sadie could uncover her own limiting beliefs she had carried with her far too long. From looking at interactions with her parents to different conversations with others, Sadie was able to recognize what she thought to be different pieces of "circumstantial evidence" for why she believed she was not lovable—something she says would cause anyone depression.

"I was living my life defined by the fact I thought I was unloved. Those were definitely the core beliefs I uncovered, and those take work every single day," Sadie said.

After working with the mental health professionals at Mclean Hospital, Sadie gradually learned to rework and redirect her thoughts through DBT. She began to stop believing the narrative in her head that her illness would stay forever. She stopped believing the narrative that no one would ever love her. She began to walk into this wisdom with open arms. She began to unpack the limiting beliefs perverting the way she saw herself and the world. Most importantly, she began to love herself through this new chapter of her life.

Sadie went on to talk about the importance of recognizing your thought patterns and learning to take hold of them when they start to steer down a path you don't want them to go down. But it's hard. Falling back into that pattern of self-loathing, worry, or fear can happen in the blink of an eye if you're not careful. Both Sadie and I know that all too well.

"If you're not paying attention to your inner monologue, if you're not paying attention to your interactions and the reasoning behind them, it's very easy to fall back into that pattern. Because for me, my instinct is to believe I don't deserve love and to interact with people based on that belief," Sadie explained. "Mental health is a lifelong struggle and a lifelong journey, and you have to be intentional about it to see the effects and to reap the benefits."

Intentionality is key in any area of life, and especially when it comes to maintaining your mental and emotional wellbeing. Like Sadie, I talked to an old classmate of mine, Leila Noghrehchi, about her struggles with mental health, especially as a current medical student.

As someone who has a brother in medical school, I have seen the immense mental, emotional, and physical hoops these med students must jump through to simply stay afloat. It's not for the weak of heart. But hearing Leila's experience firsthand gave me an even greater look into the world of mental health as a woman in the medical field, a field that is riddled with intensity, stress, and an occasional splash of blood.

"Pretty much all through college," Leila explained, "I felt okay because . . . the people around me, who also have high-functioning anxiety, were all kind of doing the same. It wasn't until medical school, where my academic self-esteem and imposter syndrome and my high-functioning anxiety—now turned baseline generalized anxiety—started to kick in."

Leila's struggles during medical school compounded over a period of time. From being one of the youngest students in her class to struggling with her studies, Leila began to feel her world crashing down upon her.

"I failed my first attempt at my board exam—which, for anybody who's not in medicine, it's not the end of the world. It just feels like it is." Leila explained her mental state in that moment by saying, "Everything kind of set in.... My depression and anxiety had reached a point where I had self-sabotaged on a very big part of my career, and I was met with a lot of feelings of failure and feelings like I didn't deserve to be there."

While struggling with depression and mental illness can be a difficult path for many, being a woman in a fairly masculine field can feel isolating and rejecting. "I saw around me women or medical students [who] were successful in managing their emotions and did not need to see a therapist or seek help out somewhere else," Leila described. "I don't know if there's just something about being a woman and then being diagnosed with depression and anxiety.... You're almost put into a box.... You're just another woman in her mid-twenties dealing with anxiety and depression."

While it's sad, it's unfortunately true. Young women—particularly in their teens and twenties—are susceptible to developing mental illness, often due to external factors like sexual abuse, alcohol, drugs, work, relationships, or childhood traumas. According to the American Addiction Centers, nearly three-fourths of all chronic mental illnesses develop by the age of twenty-four years old. So, while people like Sadie, Leila, and myself can feel isolated, confused, and frustrated by these fairly true stereotypes of being a depressed teen or young adult, we are far from being the strange anomaly often associated with mental illness and young women.

Getting over the shame and hush-hush nature surrounding mental illness can be incredibly difficult, especially in a field where you are supposed to be the one taking care of others. But Leila found that becoming intentional with her mental health and getting over that mental barrier of being a simple statistic allowed her to begin her healing journey.

"I started attending these mind-body skills groups, which are offered through the Center of Mind-Body Medicine. The first time I did it, I felt great!" Leila exclaimed. "I was allocating two hours every week, just for myself and nobody else, and I was building connections with people I would never have otherwise."

It was there in her online skills group where Leila had begun to take the steps needed to heal. From managing her anxious thoughts to fixing her GI-related issues due to her anxiety, Leila mentioned putting herself first and walking into a space where she can remain present and intentional with her current state of mind are key factors for her own mental health journey.

She ended our conversation by explaining a tried-and-true fact when it comes to beginning one's own mental health journey: ask for help, specifically professional help. While family, friends, and loved ones are an integral part of one's journey of healing, trained medical professionals have the ability to provide unbiased opinions and objective views on someone's mental state.

"I think hearing somebody that you don't know give you honest advice and an honest opinion about where you are mentally and how you're functioning is probably one of the most valuable pieces [of advice]," Leila said. "It's really easy for things just [to] go unnoticed for a really long period of time because everyone around you is the same."

Coming out of depression, anxiety, or any kind of other mental health-related issue is tough. It's draining. You feel like another statistic, yet so misunderstood. You want to ask for help yet are afraid. Or perhaps you just understand the gravity of the amount of work you will need to put in to overcome whatever mental struggle you are facing. I, for one, understand, as do Sadie and Leila. Recovering from mental illness often feels like an uphill battle. Like Sadie mentioned, it's a lifelong journey. But remaining intentional, reworking your thoughts, and talking to a therapist or other experts are great ways to start.

It's also important to remember mental illness is just that—an illness. It's an illness and should be treated like one. Recently, my therapist asked me: If you were a diabetic, you would go the doctor and take all the medicine you needed, right? Well, the same goes for mental illness. There is never and should never be shame in asking for help. It might feel like a problem, but there is always a solution. Always.

So, ask for help. It's never too late to start.

CHAPTER TEN

POST-GRAD & A PANDEMIC

―

Lying on the soft carpet in the corner of my living room, I feel the weight of my world pin me down to the ground. I'm unable to move. Tears begin to stream down my face, and I begin to cry. It's that kind of cry that comes from the unknown depths within, startling, loud, and all-encompassing. It's terrifying and cathartic, yet emotionally exhausting. My mother's arms wrap around me and she holds me, wiping the tears from my cheeks. I continue to bawl for the next hour. The pain deep within me seems to be unshakable and relentless, but after the tsunami of tears, I just lie there, numb.

This is depression.

As much as I want to say this happened long, long ago, I can't. This was January 2021, and while I wish I could say my depressive and anxious episodes are a thing of the past, that is simply not the case. Mental illness is funny that way. It has ebbed and flowed in and out of my life for the past ten years, and it's truly a nasty thing. Right when you think you're over it, it creeps in like a thief in the night. But regardless of its presence in my life, I make it my priority to find the silver lining in the pain of it all.

At that moment, I was going through a lot of major life changes. I started off 2021 extremely hungover (can anyone else relate?). But when my four-day hangover only seemed to get worse, I started to get worried. So, on January 5, I booked an appointment for a rapid test for the coronavirus. Sure enough, I tested positive for COVID-19. The next day, I got a call from my boss telling me the company was making layoffs, and I was included.

With the loss of my job also came the loss of my paycheck, and California is *expensive*. Because one of my 2021 goals is to become the reincarnation of Carrie Bradshaw and move to New York City (which is even more expensive than California), I had some major money-saving goals to hit. So, lying there sick and sad on my couch, I made the decision to move back to Arizona with my family for the next few months. At first, this decision felt easy to make. I was excited to be living rent-free in my parents' house for the next few months. Because Arizona still has much of its "Wild West" mentality, everything was pretty much open. I could finally start going to the gym again and eating at some of my favorite restaurants—while being COVID conscious, of course. I was excited for this next, transitional chapter of my life.

But like roses, most things have their thorns. I've talked to friends, and I always seem to hear the same story from every one of them: moving back home is *hard*, especially after living on your own for five years prior. When you move home, you begin to remember the past versions of yourself you would rather forget. You have certain memories that would be better kept locked up. But unfortunately, moving home often unearths these memories and experiences. My situation was no different. Like I mentioned before, mental health struggles come in waves. For some, this grief and pain began amidst the pandemic. For others like myself, this grief and pain came long after the initial start.

MENTAL HEALTH DURING THE PANDEMIC

Back in March 2020, I was still a senior in college, and for me, the pandemic came at a critical time in my life. Just before the pandemic hit and chaos ensued, my anxiety, depression, and unresolved past sexual trauma began to resurface. During those few months leading up to March, I remember praying to God and desperately asking Him to make the world stop for a second. I needed time to just catch my breath and heal, which was incredibly difficult to do in my last semester of college—a time thought to be one of your most joyous and celebratory times of your life. About two weeks later, after I prayed that prayer, the president announced a nationwide lockdown. I swear, God answers our prayers in funny ways. Be careful what you ask for.

But in all seriousness, the pandemic gave me time to heal. I started seeing a therapist who specialized in sexual trauma, started reading more, learned what it meant to truly trust God amidst chaos, stopped drinking excessively, and all in all became what I believe to be the best version of myself. I honestly wasn't dealing with all of the sudden moves and uprooting that many people my age were dealing with. I didn't have to move back home. I didn't have to subject myself to a negative living environment. I was living in a house with all my best friends, was rarely lonely, and was lucky to be in one of the most positive living situations I had ever experienced. I was thriving, in all honesty, which I say with understanding because I know that was not the consensus for people in my situation. But it never truly hit me that I had graduated college because my friends and I carried on with life as best we could, given the situation. Of course, we missed the bars, music festivals, and large crowds of sweaty people (I know you did, too). But we had each other and the beach. What more can a girl ask for?

So, while I did experience my own fair share of pain and trauma that 2020 gave all of us, I still was not dealing with the pain and trauma that comes with new beginnings, uprooting, and change. I had somehow skipped that part, until now.

Now, I feel like all the growing pains and trauma that 2020 threw at us are coming to fruition in my own life. For the first time in a really long time, I am alone. College is a beautiful thing because it is one giant community. For extroverts like myself, that was a great blessing. But now, I find myself in a state where I know only my family and one friend. I've realized I deeply and intensely miss my friends, for they are like sisters to me. I miss my morning walks around my neighborhood as I watch the kids next door rush out the door to school. I miss walking along the sand of the Pacific Ocean, talking to God, listening to music, and feeling the cool, salty water crash against my sandy feet. For it was those moments that truly shaped me into the person I am today. For the first time since March 2020, I feel like it's now my turn to grieve what once was, to cry out for what is lost, and to reconcile with what is to come.

I am aware everyone deals with grief, loss, and sadness in different ways. Some, as my mother calls them, are more "even-keeled" when it comes to emotions. They feel the feelings and get over them. I, on the other hand, am an empath, meaning I feel deeply and sense the emotional and mental state of both myself and others around me. In simpler terms, I'm overly sensitive and emotional. Growing up, I was always told to get thicker skin and to stop being so sensitive. While I think it's good to let negative comments and hurtful things roll off of you, I do think my sensitive nature allows me to see the world in a different light. I am compassionate, thoughtful, and immensely caring. When things like grief, loss, and sadness come into my life, they come into my life in full force.

While I could say I am an anomaly for being so emotional, I know that is not the case. Mental health has been a buzz-worthy topic for a while now, but since the start of the pandemic, mental health has been top of mind for many. When the lockdown initially happened, my mind immediately went to how this global situation would affect everyone's mental sanity. I mean, being locked in your house is one thing. But being in this situation for over a year can be traumatizing (unless you live in Florida; I hear there are no rules there).

As stated by an academic article published in *PLOS ONE*, people experiencing mental health issues stemming from

COVID-19 are more likely to be women, Asians, students under twenty-five years old, those with poor health, those who know of someone with COVID-19, and those struggling to make ends meet financially. In a study conducted from mid-March to early May of 2020, 85 percent of the 2,534 people who participated stated they were experiencing moderate to high levels of psychological impact due to COVID-19. Though this study was conducted early in the pandemic, similar studies conducted several months in are showing similar results. A more recent study in August 2020 showed suicidal ideation among people ages eighteen to twenty-four and people experiencing anxiety has increased three-fold from the same time last year (Prior, 2020).

It's also important to note people who were white, were in the upper-middle class, spent two or more hours a day outside, and spent less than eight hours looking at a phone, computer, or television, had lower levels of psychological stress due to COVID-19. While this pandemic has burdened many with mental health-related issues, it has also shown the prevalent systematic racism, bigotry, misogyny, and classism in our nation and around the world. While I won't go into the details and logistics of these issues (as that is its own book within itself), I think it is important to note women, BIPOC, and people in the LGBTQ+ community are more prone to have negative mental and emotional health, not only because of the pandemic, but also because we unfortunately still live in a country and world that has discriminatory ideologies and laws. On the flip side, people who look like me are predisposed to have better mental and emotional health during these times, as stated prior.

As I am writing this in January 2021, this pandemic—from what experts believe—is far from over. That can be really disheartening to hear from both a personal, professional, and global perspective. I know I cannot stop the pain and hurt so many are experiencing during this time. I know I am unable to completely stop all of the injustices that have occurred and will continue to occur, as I am aware I still have a lot more to learn and unlearn. I know I cannot stop this pandemic, because let's face it, I was never really good at science and we would all be doomed if I was the one in charge.

But I can start with myself, and so can you. Like any traumatizing time in your life, you can feel alone, in pain, distraught, and confused, but there are two things you can take comfort in when feeling this way: 1) you will always have you, and 2) community is always there—sometimes you just have to look.

YOU ALWAYS HAVE YOU

Let's start with yourself. There's the saying, "You're born alone, and you die alone." Sounds depressing, because it kind of is. But it is also an absolutely beautiful thing because you get to spend a lifetime getting to know yourself. You get a lifetime growing and changing and evolving. You have a lifetime with your mind, and as someone once told me, you spend a majority of your life in your mind, so it might as well be a good place to live!

For me, spending time with myself as I grow, evolve, and change looks a lot like going on walks, reading engaging and captivating books, listening to podcasts and sermons that make me think, and looking out at the ocean after a long, hard day because it reminds me that my problems are minuscule. Spending time with myself looks a lot like searching my heart and mind for any toxic, oppressive, or false thoughts about myself and others. It looks like running, surfing, exercising, and listening to music. It is now my inner peace.

For a time, I couldn't say all of this was true. I used to spend my moments with myself in self-loathing, self-deprecation, bitterness, and loneliness. But as I've grown and matured over the years, I've learned the best way to improve your mental, emotional, and even spiritual health is by actually enjoying the precious moments with yourself. While it takes time and a whole lot of work to get to this point, it is well worth it. Personally, I have found my mindset has completely shifted from that of worthlessness to worthiness.

While I know it can sound fairly obnoxious that finding "inner peace" and learning to love and enjoy time alone are the keys to living a happier and healthier life, science has confirmed these are incredibly important when improving and maintaining a healthy mental and emotional state. According to many recent studies, developing inner peace within your own self can increase intelligence and rewire your brain to help you see the positive in life, develop more compassion for others, become more happy and joyful, improve your immune system, and improve your overall mental wellbeing (Desai, 2019).

FIND YOUR TRIBE

Though spending time with yourself is incredibly important in developing a healthy mindset and plays an integral part in combatting mental illness, community is also amazing and essential to persevering through the difficult times. I am a firm believer that we as human beings were meant to live in community with each other, which is definitely difficult in a time where we are encouraged to isolate and not congregate. Trust me, I miss the days of walking into crowded bars, going to church, and attending a yoga class where we were all feeling the "burn" together.

If this pandemic has shown us anything, it's that we can still find community in creative ways. We saw it with the Zoom happy hours, online workouts, virtual meet ups, and online church. You name it, and you could find it virtually. Whether you find community in person or virtually, studies show finding a community has a number of positive mental health effects. The National Alliance of Mental Illness (NAMI) says the three main benefits of finding and participating in a community are belonging, support, and purpose. Community can look different to everyone. We were never designed to live in isolation, but rather with people who share similar beliefs, values, and culture. So even if we are physically isolated, we don't have to be emotionally isolated. We can foster community through virtual interaction with others and create a sense of safety for ourselves. By coming together in community, feelings of isolation, loneliness, and sadness are greatly lessened, helping to improve mental health overall. By coming together in community, we can learn and better understand each other, both crucial skills during this time of monumental change.

But let's get real, I'm fully aware that learning to balance a love for alone time and time with community will not fix everyone's mental health struggles. I am in no way trying to sugarcoat any solutions that claim to fix mental illness overnight. Like I mentioned before, mental health is a *journey*, and there's no one-size-fits-all approach. Therapy, medication, and other types of treatment are also fabulous tools and play a huge part in people's mental health journeys. But in addition to those things, I've personally found (and science has shown) that spending time finding my own inner peace and cultivating relationships with people in a trusted community have helped immensely in pulling me out of my darkest times.

Maybe you are struggling right now. Maybe it feels like the world is crashing in around you. Maybe it all feels like a little too much to handle.

Get outside. Call a friend. Reach out to loved loves. Immerse yourself in something new. Choose whatever your soul is drawn to in that moment. Whether that is to spend some time alone or in the company of others, you can find some sense of inner peace.

CHAPTER ELEVEN

ALONE OR LONELY?

Trader Joe's is honesty the best thing this world has to offer. I'm serious. It has everything you could ever want! From produce, to meats, to frozen food, to all of the incredible snacks, Trader Joe's has it all. You know what's even better? Their customer service. It's hands down my favorite outing every Sunday when I trek over to my local Trader Joe's to buy some goodies for the week and, better yet, have some quality conversations about what kind of crackers I should eat with my hummus. Their employees really give me the lowdown on what's up.

In fact, I love Trader Joe's for this sole reason: I never feel alone while I'm there. I'm surrounded by both happy employees and content customers all ready to strike up a conversation at the drop of a hat. As an introverted extrovert, being alone is something I value and despise at the same time. I need my alone time to recharge, but I also need connection. Conversation is my stimulant of choice, and when there is absolutely no one to talk to for an extended period of time, I'm left not only alone, but lonely.

Alone and lonely can be two separate things. You can be completely alone by yourself, yet so incredibly content. But there are times where your aloneness and loneliness go hand in hand. On the flip side, there've been times where I've been in a crowded room yet felt so isolated and lonely. I'm sure you've felt the same at one point or another.

Our loneliness can drive us to do a plethora of questionable things, and for me, my past loneliness has driven me to take a multitude of debatable actions, mostly relating to my past history with men. Boy after boy and one brief relationship after the other, I spent most of my college years searching for someone and something that could fill the void. I wanted something that would make the dull, dark feeling go away. I was on the hunt to fix this problem I had. But was it really even a problem?

I remember sitting on my dorm couch one night during my sophomore year, I could feel the loneliness crawl up my spine, waiting to remind me I was alone once again. In desperate need of someone or something to take away my loneliness, I dove at any opportunity that allowed me to forget my deep-rooted issues at hand. I've always struggled with my insecurity around being single. From the time I had my first crush at the sweet and innocent age of five years old, I've longed to be in a relationship. What can I say, I'm a hopeless romantic. But after years of pursuing boys with emotional immaturity and commitment issues, I still have spent a majority of my twenty-three years on this earth as a single woman. As someone who has been the perpetual third wheel for all my friends, I was often left to be reminded of my singleness, which only allowed my loneliness to grow deeper.

Fast forward one year, and I am sitting on my tiny IKEA couch in Rome. It is dark outside, the weather is absolutely horrendous, and I am all alone. I could feel those lonely shivers crawl up my spine once again, there to remind me of my isolation. In this season of my life, I felt like I was stranded on some foreign island, unable to escape, never to be saved from outside forces. A few months prior to moving to Italy for my study abroad experience, I had experienced my first true heartbreak that honestly broke me, was coping with my recent rape, and to top it all off, got a concussion two months before leaving for Italy. To stay on trend, I decided to add this new little injury to my list of things to forget. Unfortunately, concussions don't work like that. They're kind of like God; they demand to be noticed.

So there I was, sitting on my couch all alone, ten thousand miles away from any kind of normalcy, and still concussed. The only difference? I didn't have men to temporarily wash the pain away. I had wine for that. Rosé soon became a friend of mine and temporarily drowned out the pain I was dealing with, both physically and emotionally. I was utterly depressed at this point and denying all my feelings, only making everything worse. I thought for a while if I could just pretend everything was okay, eventually it would be. But just like the theoretical masks we often wear, my denial was only a filter for my feelings. In the moment, it was less painful to pretend than to face my issues.

I remember one of my last days in Rome sitting in my favorite American-esque coffee shop. I was attempting to study for my final when the deepest sense of despair washed over me. There I was, a blonde American girl from California, bawling in the cafe near the corner all alone. I put sunglasses on in hopes no one would notice, but it felt as if everyone was staring. I remember praying to God, wondering why I was struggling so damn much.

Was this normal? Why was it so much easier for everyone to be happy? Why couldn't I be like everyone else?

While in those moments it felt like my world was falling apart, it was actually falling together. Walking home from the cafe that rainy December day down those sparkling cobblestone roads, I made a promise to myself to heal. I would heal all the hurt and pain I had accumulated over the years. I promised to heal my body physically so I could go through life without crippling migraines every morning and night, to heal my soul from past toxic relationships. It's in those moments of feeling utterly helpless and painfully in despair when you can turn the page of your own narrative and walk into something truly awe-inspiring.

It was in the months after my study abroad experience where I learned to get comfortable in my loneliness. I spent hours a week talking to God, walking, listening to sermons, and discovering how the human condition was divinely created to be. I learned my loneliness was my fog, something that shielded my eyes from seeing my own truth and my own insecurities. I had been wearing this theoretical mask, covering my own pain with a flimsy facade.

Similar to loneliness, I believe any intense emotion is trying to communicate with us. Oftentimes we are standing in our own way. So disillusioned by our own fog, we are simply confused when these waves of emotions wash over us. Rather than question what we are feeling and dissect every thought we have, we numb the pain. We call that ex, we take the pill, throw back another bottle. We live in a society where we spend so much time running away from the pain that we end up running straight into it, especially in an era of social media.

We've all fallen victim to that late-night scroll through our feed. You had a long day. You want to numb your brain for just a bit. But what does that scrolling actually do? In a recent online publication from the University of Nevada, Reno, 20 percent of young adults who have at least one social media account feel the need to check up online to distract themselves and avoid any potential generalized anxiety that might occur. This act of constant checking in on social media can take FOMO, or the fear of missing out, to a whole new level.

In a 2019 study done by Common Sense Media, 54 percent of teens using social media admits to scrolling their social media feeds while talking with others, rather than actively listen during the conversation. This statistic has grown by 10 percent since 2012. With the increased use of social media, experts have linked social media use to an increase in mental illness and sleep deprivation, as well as a decline in overall physical health over the past few years (Northwest Primary Care, 2021).

Scarier yet, mental illness in relation to social media and technology use has increased quite a bit since the introduction of smartphones back in 2007. According to the Child Mind Institute, depressive symptoms in eighth- to twelfth-grade children have increased by 33 percent in 2017. Between 2010 and 2015, suicide increased by a whopping 65 percent in this age group. Both statistics have been shown to highly correlate with the adoption of social media and technology.

Now let's throw COVID-19, political tension, and civil unrest into the mix. We have a recipe for disaster. As of late June 2020, about 40 percent of Americans were dealing with mental health or substance-related issues. About 10.7 percent of people said they have thoughts of suicide, which is up from 4.3 percent twelve months before (CDC, 2020). Another way people are again running away from their depression and anxiety? Alcohol! From March to June 2020, alcohol sales in America rose by 27 percent (Valinsky, 2020).

It's easy to cloud our minds with these different distractions or substances in hopes of running away from our present reality. No one ever sat us down when we were growing up and said, "Here are three easy steps to survive a global pandemic." No one really knows what the hell we are doing—pandemic or not. All reactions are valid. But the important thing to remember here is not all reactions are healthy and conducive for your mental, emotional, and spiritual health.

We are being conditioned by society to run to the things that numb our minds, whether that be alcohol, sex, social media, or a combination of all three. I'm scared that we'll soon live in a world where unplugging is a thing of the past, self-discovery is obsolete, and stillness is no longer seen as needed. I often look around and feel like I am surrounded by people lost in another reality. I can sense it in the eyes of the young girl walking down the street. I can sense it as I have a brief conversation with a peer or colleague. They have this glassy look that falls over their eyes, lifeless and limp. Even more frightening, sometimes I can feel myself being sucked into that alternate reality as well, the alternate reality where numbing anything and everything is simpler than feeling the gravity of it all.

But that's when I remind myself. I turn to God, I pray, and I experience nature, without the distractions of any technology. These are the things that keep my soul feeling alive and not drained from the negativity swirling around me. I honestly thank God for my extended struggles with loneliness, for I was able to learn how to become in tune with my emotional and spiritual wellbeing. I was able to take a step back from my everyday life and question why I truly felt this way. My "aloneness" no longer made me lonely. Rather, it allowed me to spend uninterrupted time with myself and the Divine. I took myself on dates, wined and dined myself, went to yoga, sat on the sand, and did things alone that brought me a sort of reprieve from the chaos in my mind and from the outside world. It was in those moments of unplugging, reassessing, and centering that I was able to transform my mind and lift the fog from my own conscience.

I recently read a book by John Mark Comer titled *The Ruthless Elimination of Hurry*. This book was gifted to me by my friend Nadine Krill, and it came to me when I needed it the most. It's funny how life does that. It sends you books, people, and another blessing in the nick of time.

As I was reading one morning, I came across this phrase: "Solitude is engagement; isolation is escape. Solitude is safety; isolation is danger" (Comer, 2019).

It got me thinking. Maybe I was confusing my loneliness with self-inflicted isolation?

Comer goes on to state: "One of the greatest problems of spirituality in our day and age that so few people feel safe enough to admit is how separated we feel from God. We rarely experience God's presence throughout our day. . . . Often we come to church hoping for a God hit—a fleeting moment of connection to God before we return to the secular wasteland." I think we all can grudgingly admit we feel a little disconnected from time to time. We use our Friday nights to escape our jobs. We spend hours on the internet secretly jealous of that person with the amazing body and massive yacht. We deep dive into distraction after distraction and are left feeling disconnected from God and even ourselves.

In all honesty, I'm the queen of doing this. I've always been the person who is an overachiever. I'm a three wing two according to the Enneagram test, which basically means I love overachieving and I am emotional. Let me tell you, that is me in a nutshell. I oftentimes break my back to accomplish all I have set out to be.

For example, I currently am the podcast manager for three different podcasts, have my own podcast where I create all my content and post weekly, and am writing this book, which is a job within itself. I am also a national qualifying triathlete, and since exercise is another form of breathing to me,

I always set aside time for at least one hour a day to work out. I usually work seven days a week and often have several mental breakdowns every month. Is that healthy? Probably not. Is that how I cope? Absolutely.

All jokes aside, I do pride myself on being a hard worker and I wouldn't have it any other way. I love what I do, and I have some big freaking dreams I'm trying to chase over here. But for the longest time, I think I was using my workaholic nature as a form of self-medicating, distraction, and disconnection from reality. I was trying to run away from my uncomfortable feelings of loneliness by out-working everyone around me. Maybe they would love me more if I did what everyone thought I couldn't do? Maybe *I* would love *me* more?

I think oftentimes we as humans feel so far away from God, the universe, the source—whatever you want to call it—making us lost and passionless. As a Christian, I think God is constantly calling us back to Him, often in the most subtle ways. I think we believe we can do this life all on our own, without the help of anyone or anything to get us by. When we realize we actually can't do half the things we set out to do on our own, we panic. We retreat. We try so freaking hard to hold it all together, just to see it all slip through our fingers.

I think that's when we become truly lonely and isolated. We do it to ourselves, and we're left there sitting alone, crying and in pain.

So, what if we could change our loneliness and isolation into solitude? What if the path out of our own personal hell is just shifting our perspective by two degrees?

I've seen this two-degree shift in my own life, and it has changed everything. What used to be my days alone are now my quiet moments with God. What used to be my sad Friday nights by myself are now spent basking in the fact that I am my own best friend. What used to be the days I spent listening to sad R&B music are now me blasting Lizzo, happy as can be.

My point is, I've used this time in my life to embrace my loneliness and reflect on all my emotions (with the help of therapy, of course). I've learned to switch my perspective from one full of loneliness and isolation to one full of solitude and gratitude. I'm slowly but surely learning to change that mindset and cultivate a work ethic based on love and passion, rather than approval. I view my solitude as my anchor, my safe place for when life seems to be getting out of hand. My solitude is the thing that saved me from my loneliness. It's as if I watched the clouds that once surround me dissipate with every quiet time, every prayer, and every meditation on God's Word.

I've never been so fulfilled in my life. To be alone and content. What a concept.

CHAPTER TWELVE

VALIDATION IS FOR PARKING

―

Is there ever a moment where Carrie Bradshaw is wrong?

Six months into quarantine, I decided I needed to develop a mindless pastime. I've never really been one for Netflix binges, as I simply find them a waste of time. As an Enneagram three, I am the "overachiever," and I wear that title proudly. But even I have grown tired of my workaholic tendencies lately. My life is mundane.

Wake up.
Eat.
Work.
Become increasingly irritated with my boss.
Workout.
Eat.
Cry.
Eat.
Work more.

Drink wine.
Sleep.
Repeat.

I knew post-grad life was going to be rough but doing it in a pandemic is another story. Desperate to change it up a little, I decided to watch *Sex & the City*. With my lackluster love life, maybe this was the thing I needed to transport me back into the days where dating didn't seem deadly and falling in love actually seemed like a possibility.

I've grown to admire Carrie's way with words. She's inspired much of my writing and watching the show makes me dream of the day I'll be living in New York, successful and single—maybe I'll have a man by then, but that is to be determined.

Tonight is Christmas, and I am sitting here with ice cream on my right and a tequila soda on my left—very festive if I do say so myself. It is my fifth night in a row watching *Sex & the City,* and I am thoroughly enjoying every second of my new mindless pastime. While every episode seems to be riddled with thought-provoking statements, tonight Carrie said something so profound I literally squealed:

> Why is it that we only seem to believe the negative things people say about us? No matter how much evidence there is to the contrary—a neighbor, a face, an ex-boyfriend can cancel out everything we thought was once true. But when it comes to life and love, why do we believe our worst reviews? — (*Sex and the City*, 2002).

It got me thinking: why do we seek validation from everyone but ourselves? It seems like a disease that plagues our society. With every like, every view, and every repost, our quest for external validation has only grown bigger and bigger, eventually suffocating us with the opinions and judgments of others.

According to Dictionary.com, validation "is the act of affirming a person, or their ideas, feelings, actions, etc., as acceptable and worthy." Validation looks like: "I hear you. I'm listening. That must be hard. I understand." To provide validation, you do not necessarily have to agree with the person, rather just affirm the other's opinions or feelings.

Validation promotes recognition and acknowledgment and leads to acceptance and understanding. In fact, validation is incredibly important in one's formative years, as it helps to create an emotionally safe environment for children to flourish and allows children to learn appropriate behaviors (McMahan, 2017). According to psychotherapist Karen R. Koenig, LCSW/MEd, children who seek and receive validation flourish emotionally, but when it comes to adults the inverse can be expected. While external validation is important when taking "instruction and constructive criticism from others to collaborate with peers, it becomes an issue when validation becomes the end all be all."

While there's nothing wrong with enjoying a well-placed compliment occasionally, an unhealthy obsession with external validation can be incredibly harmful to anyone. An unhealthy obsession with external validation can look like avoiding confrontation of any kind, changing your thoughts or opinions when someone has differing thoughts or opinions, and determining your own self-worth based on the validation of others.

Dr. Risa Stein, professor of psychology at Rockhurst University in Missouri, states, "If our life plans or even just short-term goals are guided by external criteria . . . without a true understanding of what it is that we actually want or what fulfills and satisfies us, then we end up at minimum disconcerted and unhappy, and at worst, with a midlife crisis or severely depressed" (Saline, 2019).

Does this sound like anyone you know? We all know a person, whether it be your mom, aunt, sister, best friend, or even yourself, who seems to be aimlessly living life and riding on the coattails of anyone and everyone who provides them with a sliver of praise. We've all been there at one point or another, but the key is to never stay there.

For much of my life—as I have mentioned previously—I've struggled with feeling seen. Therefore, external validation became my crutch, especially during my early college years. Every boy who told me I was pretty, I secretly swooned over. Every teacher who gave me an A, I felt a sense of pride rush over me. Every follower I gained on Instagram, I felt my head inflate one more inch. Looking back, I'm disappointed I looked for validation from people who barely even knew me and am saddened by the fact these sources of validation are so incredibly shallow.

Like I mentioned before, there is nothing wrong with validation. It's important for our mental and emotional health. But when we place such a heavy emphasis on who thinks what about us, we give up some of our own power and place it in the hands of others. By seeking validation from everyone and everything, we no longer take complete ownership over ourselves. Instead, we are now living our life to seek approval.

It truly makes my heart hurt knowing so many other younger (and even older) women are doing the same as I once did. I based my confidence on what others said of me rather than what I thought of myself or who God said I am. While it would be easy to say I've completely grown out of this need for external validation, that would be far from the truth. My deepest fear in life is disappointing my family—as it is for many others. I've always felt this deep desire to make them proud and to be the person they want me to be. Even when they tell me I am allowed to be the person I want to be, my mind still manages to convince me otherwise.

WHY BE BEIGE WHEN YOU WERE BORN TO BE RED HOT?

It's in those moments of feeling the need to live up to some imaginary sense of self that we can all lose our spark. In a podcast episode with Haley Hoffman Smith, Black female entrepreneur and founder of Money Movers International, LLC. Allyson Byrd said she perceived smallness as a consequence of mediocrity, and in return, mediocrity as a consequence of conformity. We live in a world where being the same or like others is valued. Byrd hit the nail on the head when she said:

> I perceive conformity, as a direct partner to sameness and smallness, and quite frankly being beige, when we were

all born to be red hot. I feel like so much of our society is diseased ... by being forced to be the same, and that disease shows up in our frustration in our anxiety and our mental disorders. It shows up in so many unique ways. It shows up in our autoimmune system, it shows up in arthritis, fibromyalgia, migraines. ... There is a collective consciousness that has now been born, multiple generations of people who are not themselves. When we are not ourselves, we are not fully operating in our purpose (Byrd, 2.30).

When we receive validation from others, we are validated for the parts of ourselves that are considered socially acceptable. We are positively reinforced to conform, to mold, and to act the same as everyone else. How has your need for validation caused you to conform, or to put it bluntly, how has your need for validation killed a part of your soul, your passion, or your dream? Why do we too often choose to be beige when we were born to be red hot?

I, like Allyson Byrd, believe it is because we are so focused on receiving validation from others that it becomes easier to let certain parts of yourself die, rather than spend the time fighting for them to live. Validation has become our drug of choice, and by choosing to fit our fluid passions and dreams into a premade mold, we are choosing to live a life of mediocrity. The worst part of it all is that we do this to ourselves. In her nationally acclaimed bestseller *Untamed*, Glennon Doyle touches on the fact women are taught to abandon themselves and seek validation, particularly from men.

She says, "The epitome of womanhood is to lose one's self completely" (Doyle, 2020). We forget our passions, forget our purpose, and fall into a life that others think is acceptable. We let a piece of ourselves die to fit the expectations of others, in fear of what they might think. We turn to vices to fill voids we were created to fill ourselves. We turn to booze and boys, drugs and people, overstimulation and external validation. We begin to believe this external validation will bring peace, when in all actuality, it brings chaos. We are so quick to abandon ourselves if that means someone will give us their thoughts and opinions in exchange. It's become transactional. In this transaction, we lose something so vital to our being: our future.

My relationship with and need for validation has been quite a funny one. There are days when I am feeling on top of the world, feeling fully confident in my skin, and looking for no source of external validation but from myself. But on the contrary, there are days or weeks when I'm riddled with self-doubt and seeking any and every kind of validation I can find. This is normal, but as I've grown, my need for consistent external validation has shifted. I no longer seek most of the validation from my peers or random people on the internet, but rather from my immediate family and friends. While this can be seen as a positive shift, I would still argue I give too much power to the thoughts and concerns of the ones closest to me. It's only natural to seek the most validation from your friends and family, but sometimes their thoughts and concerns can cloud your own judgment and act as their own kind of mental noise or distraction. There's a fine line between accepting and receiving validation from your loved ones and letting it be the be all end all. But when you're young like me, sometimes this fine line can be blurred.

As much as I've tried to set boundaries for myself and others when it comes to receiving and relying on validation, a part of me is always seeking that praise or compliment from my friend or family member. To be honest, I couldn't tell you why. Perhaps it's because I am still trying to figure exactly what I want to do with my life. Perhaps it's because I'm only twenty-three years old and don't have a clear vision of how to accomplish everything my heart is set on. Perhaps I still don't trust myself. Perhaps I still haven't managed to develop a consistent level of self-worth. Perhaps it's a mixture of everything.

While it can be easy to stay in this cycle of seeking others' approval, it's imperative that we learn to cut the ties from these external factors, for the risk of losing ourselves is far too great. After all, to quote Byrd, "validation is for parking, not for living." Yes, ma'am!

LEARNING TO SELF-VALIDATE

How do you being to rely on your own validation, rather than external validation? It all starts with learning to self-sustain. Some good old-fashioned self-reflection is here to help. First, meditate on your professional or academic achievements. What are they? How do they make you feel? What do others think about your achievements? Feel free to write down any things that come to mind. Next, what fulfills you personally? Is it an activity or a relationship you have? Where does this personal fulfillment come from? Write it down. Now, once you've meditated on both aspects of your life, see how both things are intertwined. Are you trying to achieve that certain thing in your professional life because you've always felt called to it or because your family has always pressured you down that path? Are you trying to lose weight because it is on trend or because you truly want to live a healthier lifestyle?

Another way to break free from the need for external validation is becoming intentional about setting aside some time for self-reflection. Too often we seek others' thoughts and opinions on a subject, rather than ask ourselves what we really think. Self-validation is essential and is crucial for breaking the cycle of external validation, which in turn can create a life of fulfillment and true purpose. The first step in creating space for self-validation is to simply make the time. Take yourself on a date, a walk, or a long drive. Create some alone time with yourself to simply think and reflect. The second step is to cultivate the right mindset. As women, we often aren't taught how to properly believe in ourselves and our abilities, especially in a world that tells us we must look, exist, and act a certain way. We are taught from an early age to seek applause and get the gold star. But as we grow older, we no longer see those same forms of validation we saw as children, so we struggle to make sense of this new world we live in. How are we expected to suddenly transition out of that mentality? We were never taught to give ourselves permission before anyone else gives us that permission in return. Therefore, cultivating the right mindset around self-validation as women is critical for our overall mental and emotional wellbeing.

CLAP FOR YOURSELF

I recently sat down with my mentor, Allee Williams. Allee is a serial Christian entrepreneur and someone I greatly admire. As we were talking, her words practically reverberated in my ears, as what she said was so applicable to my life at that moment in time.

She said, "I remember two years ago hearing the quote, 'You have to clap for yourself before anyone else does.' I remember being like, 'No! I want other people to clap for me!' And . . . now, you know, years later, I'm like, 'Why would someone clap for me if I am not sold on what I'm doing?'"

She went on to mention how so many young women bypass and downplay their own value. We have developed this mindset of "oh well, I'm kind of good" and "I can maybe help with x, y, and z." But why would anyone want to help you with anything if you don't even believe in your own abilities? Why would they push you to move to that big city and follow your dreams if you are so uncertain of your own decision?

Our insecure mindsets inhibit us from walking into all we are created to be. Rather than have this insecure and under-valued mindset, why not change your own narrative? As Allee exclaimed, we should say, "'Hey! I could change your life. If you say yes, then congratulations! If you say no, I'll see you later.' I think it's so important . . . to give yourself permission first and foremost. And as young women, we get to do that, and it's a freaking cool blessing. And cultivating that space, that's what helps you grow, and no one taught me that, you know?"

Cultivating the mindset of self-worth and self-value is key to minimizing one's need for external validation, but that's easier said than done. How can you start your own personal journey for creating a healthy mindset and self-esteem? Personally, I have found the use of daily, spoken affirmations an integral part of building and cultivating a healthy mindset.

According to a study done by the University of Pennsylvania back in 2015, researchers found self-affirmations activate the reward center of the brain or, more specifically, the ventral striatum (VS) and ventromedial prefrontal cortex (VMPFC). These areas of the brain are the same areas that are triggered by more pleasurable experiences, like eating a fabulous meal or winning the lottery (I can only hope and dream for the latter). In addition, the medial prefrontal cortex (MPFC) and posterior cingulate cortex (PCC), the areas of the brain related to processing personal experiences, increase in activity with self-affirmations. With an increase in activity in these areas, your brain is better able to process any "kind of emotionally painful, negative, or threatening information."

Self-affirming, after consistent and intentional work, can help transform your mindset when it comes to seeking validation from others. While daily affirmations are my personal choice for improving my self-worth and self-confidence, there are many other things you can do to stop the need for others' opinions and thoughts in your life. You can journal, meditate, or practice a skill on your own that you want to get better at. You can do a little social media cleanse. Unfollow, block, or mute—whatever you must do to resist the urge of external validation or negative naysayers. But the most important thing you can do? Simply stop asking for other's opinions or approval. I know, it might be an automatic reflex for some, but refraining from asking their thoughts and opinions gives less of a chance that they'll actually tell you.

Who knows? If you try some of these things, you might just become more confident and self-assured—a beautiful thing we all deserve as women.

CHAPTER THIRTEEN

WOMEN IN THE WORKPLACE: LACK OF CONFIDENCE & GENDER BIASES

What does it take to be the world's youngest self-made female billionaire and CEO?

For Spanx's founder and CEO Sara Blakely, it took innovation, grit, and a sense of humor.

At twenty-seven, Blakely was in a dead-end job selling fax machines door to door, had $5,000 in savings, had never worked in fashion or apparel, and had never taken a single business class. To top it all off, she had just moved out of her mother's house and was dating a loser—her words, not mine.

"I just simply wanted to wear white pants to a party and have nothing show underneath it. I spent all my hard-earned money on this one pair of cream pants that hung there, and I decided to cut the feet out of control top pantyhose one day, and I threw them on under my white pants and went to the party. I looked fabulous, I felt great, I had no panty lines, I looked thinner and smoother, but they rolled up my legs all night. I remember thinking, '*This should exist for women*'" (Blakely, 2011).

With her ideas brewing in her head and a need in the market, Blakely decided to take the next steps of creating her vision by making a patent. Blakely sought help from lawyers in creating her patent, but after presenting her so-called revolutionary idea to a room full of men, they weren't sold. During a presentation at a law firm, one attorney kept looking around the room while she was speaking. For a moment, Sara was confused.

"Was he making fun of me?" she thought.

He was. He later told her, "Sara, I thought when I first met you that your idea was so bad, I thought you had been sent by *Candid Camera*." With that statement, Sara decided to make the patent herself.

While making her own patent, Sara set out to learn a bit more about the hosiery and undergarment industry. After scouring the internet for more information on hosiery mills, Blakely soon found most undergarments for women were made in North Carolina . . . by men.

"It dawned on me maybe that's why our pantyhose had been so uncomfortable for so long—because the people making them aren't wearing them, and if they are, they're not admitting it" (Blakely, 2011).

Desperate to get more people on board with her idea, Blakely took a week off work and drove from one hosiery mill to the next, knocking on each and every door, trying to get a foot in the door and looking for potential manufacturers. However, as a woman with absolutely no financial backing, she was turned away. Disappointed, Blakely made her way back to Atlanta.

Two weeks later, she got a call from an owner at one of the mills she went to. Originally, he had turned her away, believing her idea was nothing but a hoax. But after talking to his two daughters, he called Blakely back, only to say, "Sara, I have decided to help make your crazy idea."

Ready to make her first prototype, Sara began to meet with the men in charge of the mill.

"I remember the moment specifically. I was standing in the manufacturing plants surrounded by men who make our undergarments. I thought, *'I don't have the most experience, I don't have the most money, but I do care the most. Let me see what happens if I care the most'*" (Blakely, 2020).

I think as women, we're always being told "no" in some form or capacity: "No" to dressing in a certain way; "no" to starting our own business; "no" to being a working mom; "no" to standing up for ourselves.

"No" has become a part of our auditory vernacular. Sara Blakely's initial struggles to launch her business in a male-dominated field are not unique by any means. Men dominate the entrepreneurial field tenfold.

According to a 2019 Columbia Business School study, female-led ventures are 63 percent less likely to receive venture capital funding. In a similar study, 24 percent of women don't think women will ever have equal access to capital (Score, 2020). In fact, during the *Wharton Business Daily* podcast, Ethan Mollick, a Wharton management professor at the University of Pennsylvania, stated:

If you look overall at the chance of someone starting a company, it turns out that gender is a really strong predictor of whether or not they will become an entrepreneur. Women are less likely to be entrepreneurs than men, and this has been a big puzzle, because women are as innovative [as men and] companies run by women are as successful. So why aren't women launching companies at the same rate?

Good question, Ethan. I was wondering the same damn thing!

It's no question that women are treated differently than men, especially in different cultures and countries. This disparity of women in entrepreneurship can be attributed to a million factors, including lack of confidence, societal pressures, cultural pressures, and gender norms.

But overall, I think women get caught up in being perfect—the perfect mother, the perfect daughter, the perfect sister, the perfect friend. Women of any age can become so engulfed in living a life pleasing to others that we forget our own dreams we once had so long ago.

What happened to your dream of being a chef? Or your dream of owning a boutique? Or your dream of being a CEO for a biotech company? Like Glennon Doyle once said in her New York Times bestselling book *Untamed*, women are so quick to abandon themselves because we are taught to be the martyrs for the people in our lives rather than be the models.

It turns out studies are finally verifying what women like Glennon Doyle knew for so long. They call it the "male hubris, female humility" effect. According to Ethan Mollick, overconfidence plays a huge role in entrepreneurship for women. When women portray lower levels of hubris, that is directly linked to lower levels of confidence. In contrast, women tend to portray higher levels of humility than men, meaning "in the face of actual success, you're less likely to attribute it to yourself and you're less likely to take advantage of it."

Due to these factors relating to humility, hubris, and confidence, women are less likely to try again when initially being told "no" or when they fail in acquiring enough funding. For Sara Blakely, she was an anomaly. On the other hand, men, having higher levels of overconfidence, are more willing to try something that has already failed once.

Is this effect why so many women have been afraid of failing for so long? Because we simply don't believe enough in our ability to succeed and accomplish what we set out to do?

In a sample study referred to in Include-Empower.com, research found if women were just as overconfident, immodest, and unhumbled as men, there would be 30 percent more female founding attempts. However, these qualities come on a double-edged sword. In another study, women who "exhibit stereotypically masculine traits commonly associated with leadership like assertiveness . . . are less-liked when compared with men exhibiting the same traits." It seems we just can't get it right. We're either walking in the shadow of ourselves but wishing we could achieve our deepest desires, or we are walking fully in our own power but fighting against the lies of who we are not. If you don't try, you are seen as cooperative and kind, but you are missing out on a potential future. However, if you do try, you can be seen as a bitch or aggressive, but you are finally chasing after your dreams.

The dichotomy women face is unlike any other, making it understandable why it's easier to just sit still and shut your mouth. But if you put the double-edged sword aside for just one minute and forget the negative connotations that might come along with the success, women have a remarkable chance of "climbing the latter." If women decided to be just as aggressive, just as assertive, and just as dominating as their male counterparts, there would be a 30 percent increase in female-founded businesses, as mentioned previously. That's 30 percent more women following their dreams. That's 30 percent more women not taking "no" for an answer. Imagine the kind of world we could live in if women stopped being afraid of simply showing up. Imagine the kind of world we could live in if women in business learned to take "no" as a suggestion, but never as a definite answer.

While this disparity appears for women across all different sectors, gender bias is truly apparent in the education realm. I decided to reach out to my old English teacher from eleventh grade, Ms. Sarah Driscoll, for a multitude of reasons. The first reason was that she has undoubtedly shaped me into the writer and feminist I am today, and the second was that she is very well aware of the politics surrounding the gender biases and other disparities facing women in the education field today. It's a known fact teachers and educators often make far less than they should. According to Ms. Driscoll, "They make a 'livable wage' . . . and that's about it." While there are ways to make more money as an administrator or professor, "no one goes into education for the money."

As if the lack of pay for our educators wasn't enough, men are the ones who tend to be hired for the higher-tiered positions, meaning more men tend to hold greater positions of power than women. Again, this is not surprising. This is due to a whole host of reasons, including misogyny, male hubris, female humility effect, gender roles, etc. We see it in the government, we see it in the corporate world, and we even see it in the movies.

Did you know, according to the New York Film Academy, only 30.5 percent of the speaking parts in film are women? Did you know the average ratio for male to female actors is 2.3 to 1?
Did you know 94 percent of men lead the United States' top 500 corporations? Only 6 percent of women do, on the contrary (NBC, 2020).

Did you know according to the World Economic Forum, the United States is 208 years away from true equality (Gates, 43:00)?

Not even my daughter, grandchildren, or great-grandchildren will be able to experience the freedom that comes with complete and total gender equity. Men will continue to be the main character for decades upon decades unless we do something about it.

So, how do we confront this socially and culturally created monster? How do we speed up the painful and excruciating process? How do women even get a position of power in the first place?

During a conversation between Brené Brown and Melinda Gates, Gates noted a few tangible and practical steps to quicken the process for promoting gender equality. The first aims to limit sexual harassment and abuse in the workplace. I, like many other women, have experienced sexual harassment firsthand while at work. I have had almost every single male manager in the past three years call me a "dumb blonde" while on the job, and more disturbingly, have had a male coworker repeatedly try to touch me in inappropriate places every time he was near me. As much as I hate to admit it, I rarely ever spoke up about these things because many of these actions and comments were made by my supervisors. As for my creepy coworker, it took me months to finally tell my manager what was happening. Thankfully, after that, my coworker never talked or made eye contact with me again.

Women, unfortunately, are the most targeted for this kind of behavior in the workplace, and "if a woman is harassed in her job in the United States, she leaves at an 80 percent rate within the next two years." So it's no question why women aren't getting these higher-tiered positions in the first place. They aren't getting promoted due to the frequent job switches. Accountability is the first step in solving this complex issue. There need to be repercussions for these kinds of actions against any gender to create a safe and comfortable environment for all.

We also need to start looking at the unpaid labor policies in America, such as childcare and eldercare. Being a mom is a full-time job, and my mom has always told me if being stay-at-home was a paid job, she'd be making well over six figures. "We have to look at the unpaid labor and make sure we have good policies to help women, [like] paid family medical leave," said Melinda Gates.

In addition, there need to be more women hires in key industries like technology, finance, politics, and media. Women must have more of a say in our politics and policies, as well as be the ones to tell the stories that need to be told. While gender equality is no doubt decades away, we can hopefully propel this movement of achieving gender equality in these industries and quicken the timeline.

These step-by-step actions are critical for equality, yet there is one more action that is vital for this movement: women must advocate for themselves more, because if we don't, then no one will.

We need to create an environment that helps to "bring women up to believe in themselves from the very get-go and push hard at getting those positions, especially if [we] want them." If we continue to raise women in an environment where gender roles are continually assigned to certain jobs, we will raise women who don't reach for more. In conjunction with women advocating for themselves, we need to see this same advocation from the leading corporations in America.

Have you ever seen a corporate job advertisement specifically seeking out women? As we discussed, both Ms. Driscoll and I haven't. Hands from all sides need to be extended, from all genders.

Thankfully, women like Sara Blakely, Melinda Gates, and Sara Driscoll are helping to build confidence in women in their communities and around the world. The world we live in now is flawed. You will face gender bias, disrespectful comments, and opposition. But that shouldn't ever deter you from chasing after what you've always dreamed of doing.

As for Sara Blakely, if she never created Spanx, we might not know what it looks like for a woman to fearlessly and successfully pursue a passion and a purpose. If she would've stopped at her first "no," God only knows who the world's youngest self-made female billionaire would be. Don't stop at "no." Don't stop when your doubts become loud. Don't stop when the guys start to call you a bitch. Who knows, you might just be the next female billionaire.

CHAPTER FOURTEEN

WOMEN IN THE WORKPLACE: A NEW ERA OF ENTREPRE-ISTAS

The Office is one of the greatest shows of all time for multiple reasons: Michael Scott, the dry humor, and of course, the accurate depiction of working a mundane nine-to-five job. As someone who has worked in a few different corporate settings, I can attest to the fact that the occasional dread, weird coworkers, and tiny cubicles are not something I have a great propensity for.

Ever since I can remember, I've dreaded working a typical corporate job. More specifically, I've dreaded working in a cubicle. The stuffy environment, the uncomfortable chairs, the constant staring at a computer screen—talk about being *miserable*.

As I grew older and went to college, my university would host a career fair every semester. It was my first semester of senior year, and I was on the job hunt. I absolutely hate procrastinating, so finding a job well before I graduated was top of mind. But, in all honesty, so was partying. I was in my senior year, can you blame me? So, what seemed like any other Thursday afternoon turned out to be rather an important one—one I was not aware of.

The night before, I went out to the bars. Needless to say, I didn't wake up feeling fresh. I only had one morning class on Thursdays, so I rushed my hungover self out of bed. It was September, and San Diego is *hot*. The temperature can get into the upper nineties, and with the ocean humidity, you will be sweaty in a matter of minutes after stepping foot outside. On this day, I groggily picked up the first pair of shorts I saw and a crop top, and I made my way to class. It wasn't until I got to campus when I noticed that everyone looked nice. Girls were wearing heels and dresses, and the boys were looking fine in their suits and ties. I, on the other hand, looked like a hungover hot mess in booty shorts and a midriff top. I was able to put the dots together and realized I might have missed my chance at making a good impression with a future employer—or not.

I knew my outfit of choice that day didn't translate well to the professional world, and I understand why. It would be hard to take anyone seriously during an important interview or multi-million-dollar deal if they were barely wearing clothes. But I was also in desperate need of a job and didn't have enough time to go home and change.

So after somewhat careful consideration, I decided to bite the bullet and go to the career fair with my booty shorts and crop top. I'll admit, this wasn't my proudest moment, and I was a little self-conscious, but I was still eager to make a good impression. So, I walked into the room, faking it until I made it, shaking the hands of many, and getting as many business cards I could. Did I get any strange looks from the employers? Yes. But did I get a job interview out of it? Absolutely! While I wouldn't say wearing a similar outfit is recommended, I can say a positive and confident attitude will definitely intrigue some of the recruiters.

HOW YOUR FEMININITY IS YOUR BIGGEST STRENGTH IN THE WORKPLACE

I've always been disturbed by the lack of relaxed and laid-back energy in business. From my perspective growing up, all I ever heard about were men in suits aggressively leading business meetings and crunched over their computers for hours and hours on end. On the other hand, women were portrayed as the bitches who neglected any sort of personal life in hopes of making a living. But after I walked out of the career fair that day, a few recurring thoughts came to me: Where are all the women in business? Why does everyone look like they need to take a Xanax? Is it possible to interject some of my feminine energy into this male-dominated field? If so, how can I do it while still being taken seriously?

Apparently (thank God), I'm not the only one who thinks this way. When out at a cocktail party after the initial launching of Spanx, Sara Blakely, who I discussed previously, was approached by a few men in suits. After making some small talk, one man looked her straight in the eye and said, "You know, Sara, business is war." The men then walked away with gleaming smiles.

Later that evening, Sara sat there on the floor of her apartment and thought, *I don't want to go to war.... There's got to be a better way.* It was at that moment when Sara made the choice that so many women were yearning for: she would make business more feminine.

While there is a time a place to have masculine energy in the board room, "there hasn't been a lot of room for the feminine energy in business at all," as Sara said. "I really wanted to see if I could achieve success with honoring more of the feminine principles, and that's being vulnerable, more collaboration, and not wanting to annihilate the competition."

Some of these concepts are very foreign to some men.

So, Sara set out to see how she could serve both her customers and employees with honesty and integrity. She tried business a different way, and for her, that meant staying true to her core values of femininity.

"It literally felt almost like an experiment to myself. I was like, 'Well, let's just see if you can be successful doing it this way.'" And it's safe to say she was! While Sara doesn't only do business in a purely feminine manner, "It's very important in business and entrepreneurship to honor the balance of both the male and the feminine energy." Without the ying, you can't have the yang.

Like Sara, my former podcast guest and acquaintance, Sydney Phillips, knows exactly how important the balancing of both masculine and feminine energy is. At twenty-two years old, Sydney is a serial entrepreneur in the technology and commercial real estate space. As a past pageant queen and a fearless firecracker of a female founder, Sydney knows how to captivate a room full of investors. When asked if she gets nervous as a young female entrepreneur (or entrepre-ista as I like to call it) as she walks into a room full of older, male investors, Sydney's response was both endearing and astounding.

"I call it big sunglass energy, or BSE," she chuckled. "If you think about it, like whenever you put on those big sunglasses that cover your entire face, there's just a level of sass and attitude that you have." As someone who personally has her own pair of BSE, I can attest to this!

Before meeting with Forbes, investors, or any other bigwig CEO, Sydney says this pep talk really does the trick. She tells herself, "Alright, I'm going to walk into this room, and I'm going to be the only girl for the third week in a row in this investor meeting. I have big sunglass energy, and I'm going to be nice to everyone, and everyone's going to expect me to be mean and rude and whatever. But I'm going to be confident, but I'm also going to be kind." By bringing her feminine touch to both business and the board room, Sydney is able to feel completely herself without feeling as if she's putting on some kind of show—a quality that many women are still struggling with.

"We associate business with so many masculine traits, where I see a lot of girls try to turn into more masculine versions of themselves," Sydney mentioned. "I say, 'No!' I mean, I have literally six pink suits, and they're all different shades." Sydney's not trying to join the good ole' boys club. Rather, she's changing the game and making a new club—one that's leading the way to a better future.

FOLLOWING THE FAITH, NOT THE FEAR

Speaking of women changing the way entrepreneurship is done, Allee Williams is a female on fire for all things business and is changing the way we see our successes and failures. As mentioned previously, Allee, both my mentor and friend, is a social media marketing wiz, podcaster, and founder of the Malibu Method, a social media marketing agency that aims to help women entrepreneurs create life-changing businesses. While Allee might now have a handle on her businesses, there was once a time when Allee felt like life was coming straight at her (we've all been there before).

After taking a fifth year in college to figure out exactly what she wanted to do with her life, Allee hit a wall of confusion. "I had done it all right, always. I was always lovely and perfect and showed up and was who everyone needed me to be in whatever form." But while that facade is sustainable for a bit, it won't last in the long run. So desperate to find her own calling and purpose in life, she began doing the inner reflective work, going to therapy, and spending time with God. While the plan was to become a lawyer, life had other plans for Allee.

Toward the end of college, Allee landed an internship with Coca-Cola and helped launch a viral campaign. This campaign turned out to be "the first thing that Coke had seen from her program that was actually leveraging the attention and interaction of people" in an interactive, organic way in a while. It was at that moment when Allee realized two things: 1) she was great at social media, and 2) she wanted to be an entrepreneur. So, with her fiery nature and drive to help others, Allee decided to leave her small town in Kentucky to attend an entrepreneurship program in San Francisco and explore what life was like out West.

But while her drive and desire for more kept her going, Allee still faced some major opposition as she was ready to take the leap. Both of her parents pleaded with her to take the job at Coca-Cola and follow a path that was more "normal." While the temptation to please her family and the people around her was alive and well, Allee knew "normal" was not her calling. Confused and frustrated, Allee visited her mentor days before she was supposed to leave for San Francisco. But there was a slight problem: she needed the money to get there. After going back and forth with her mentor about whether or not she should go, her mentor said, "God can't bless you unless you show up."

So that's exactly what she did. By putting her faith in God and taking the leap, Allee created a GoFundMe campaign seventy-two hours before she was supposed to leave. In a miraculous blessing, Allee was able to raise just enough money to make her way to the West Coast and be a part of the entrepreneurship program. From there, Allee has been all around the West Coast acquiring knowledge, learning from the ups and downs of business, and relying on a lot of faith to get her through it all. From San Francisco to Scottsdale to LA, Allee grew her faith and her business by trusting that there was a greater purpose in the uncertainty.

While the entrepreneurship route isn't for everyone, it got me thinking. Why don't more women in their twenties take the risk and start a business? Why do we sit and contemplate if we should do x, y, and z, and ask every single person we know if we should pursue what's on our hearts? Why can't we take that leap of faith rather than spend those dreaded years in a masculine, corporate environment that makes our skin crawl?

From a logical standpoint, it takes a lot of money and funding to start a business. When I interviewed Karen Cahn, the founder and CEO of IFundWomen, she stated women in business are "chronically underfunded, underbanked, and generally underserved by the financial services industry." When it comes to businesses backed by venture capital, in 2020, "female-founded companies raised just 2.3 percent of the VC funding pie (a decrease from 2.8 percent in 2019). When women go to take out a bank loan, they receive lower loan amounts and higher interest rates than men." Money plays a huge factor in starting and building a proper business, and even if women have a good idea of what they want their business to be, they don't have access to the right resources. You can't blame women for not taking a leap of faith into their entrepreneurial ventures because it's simply not feasible most of the time.

From a broader and emotionally charged standpoint, I think as women we are simply afraid. We are afraid to show up for what we are called to do, afraid of failure, afraid of going against the status quo, and afraid of what others will think.

We are afraid of it all. I get it—as someone who has struggled with major anxiety, fear has been an unfortunate friend of mine. But like Sydney once told me, "Fear is an annoying friend that is just worried about you." While I don't think you can ever get rid of this annoying friend completely, you do have the choice of whether or not to let it dictate your actions.

For example, after college, I accepted an offer as a recruiter. Not my first option, but I was grateful to have a job during a pandemic. Four months in, I was itching to get out. I felt passionless and purposeless in my job, and I knew I needed to make the switch. However, the fear of quitting engulfed me. What would my parents say? What would my friends think? How would I support myself financially? These were all valid questions, but at the end of the day, I knew I couldn't stay at a job that was draining the life out of me.

So, four months into my corporate job, I called my manager and quit on the spot—both a liberating and terrifying experience to say the least. After I was a free woman, I hit the ground running. My best friend Grace says it's when you have nothing that you really have a fire lit underneath you. Boy, was she right! These past six months since quitting my job and jumping headfirst into freelancing, I've hustled harder than I ever thought possible. I've learned to ask for help, I've hit a lot of bumps in the road, I've cried more than I thought possible, and I've felt a sense of deep peace and purpose all at the same time. I'm learning to hold space for all of these emotions that ebb and flow in and out of my life every day as a young entrepreneur. I'm learning that jumping into entrepreneurship is what I am meant to do, even if that means I don't have a clear picture of the outcome.

When it comes to jumping into entrepreneurship from a financial standpoint, Karen Cahn said it best when she preached:

There are a lot of amazing men who want to see the industry change and are truly allies for women getting funded—seek them out and ask for help. Ask them to make connections for you. Ask them to write you *big checks*. Do not stand for table scraps anymore, ladies. Make bold asks because that's what our male counterparts do, and they get the money. Also, don't give up. It's on us to be the change we want to see in the world, so no matter how hard our journey as women is, don't give up.

Showing up boldly and not giving up are keys to succeeding in any business, from both a financial and personal standpoint. I don't know about you, but I want to start living my life before it's halfway over. I trust there is a greater purpose for my life, and I want to redefine the narrative that women have to be a certain way, act a certain way, and show up in life a certain way. Stepping out in faith for me means I am unapologetically myself, crop tops and all. It means I know what I want without necessarily knowing how to get there. That's why it's called taking the leap— because sometimes you won't really know the final outcome, but you trust something great will come from it.

It's my wish you will do the same—whatever that may be. Don't get bogged down by the words "no," "can't," and "won't." It's time to change your vocabulary! It's time to redefine yourself on your own terms, and not by what others say. You want to create an environment that embraces your authentic self and changes the way people think of women in the workplace? That's awesome, but you're going to have to start with yourself. You're going to have to get over the fact that others might not like that. You're going to have to take the leap anyway. You want to be the first woman to create a new market? That's sick, but you're going to have to do some things differently if you want to be different. You're going to have to take the leap.

The leaps can be scary, whether they are small or big. But faith in yourself, faith in God, and faith in a divine plan are keys to overcoming the fear, especially in entrepreneurship. We need more women in this space. Not because there are too many men, but because we have something unique to offer. We see life in a different way (they say men are from Mars, and women are from Venus for a reason). We need to ditch the stereotypes that reside in our heads and embrace ourselves as we are, because it's only when we are our truest selves that we can fully step into what we are called to be. No more pretending to be this or that. No more comparing and contemplating. Pull the damn cord and jump.

As Allee told me, "You're never going to be ready, you're never going to feel fully equipped, [and] you're never going to know all the details." There's a refining and sanctification process that comes with the journey and unknown. Allow the fear to fuel you. Allow the process to change you for the better.

Because we need you and your purpose. So step out in faith and take the freaking leap!

CONCLUSION

So, we come back to the original question: What if? What if women took the time to pause for just a moment, long enough to take inventory of their lives? What if women could walk into a version of their truest selves, confidently and unapologetically? Through the growing pains, trials, and tribulations of women's young adult lives, what if we could begin to make sense of it all?

It's stressful, after all, growing up in a society that shames us for being one thing and condemns us for being the next. All jumbled together, this can put major stress on anyone at any stage of life. How can we move forward, past the hurt, past the pain, past the experiences that shaped us for better or for worse? How can we push past and make sense of it all?

This is something I asked myself before writing this.

You see, I'm still in the thick of it as I write this book. I'm post-grad, I don't have a steady full-time job yet, I live with my parents, and I am surrounded by absolutely no one. I feel like I'm losing my mind on a daily basis, and writing about these experiences hasn't been a walk in the park.

Reliving the pain, trauma, and hurt is driving me to therapy once again because I've even realized throughout this writing process that I'm far from healed, but I'm getting there. You see, the difference between who I once was and who I am now is night and day. The girl I wrote about was insecure, lonely, and anxious beyond belief. While I might still be dealing with similar issues, I've learned better coping habits along the way. I've learned I no longer have to wait until I hit a new rock bottom to ask for help. I've learned I no longer have to validate myself based on others' opinions of me, because my opinion of myself will always be enough. I learned my body is beautifully and wonderfully made—even though I did gain the quarantine fifteen! I learned I am capable of anything I set my mind to, even if a man laughs and tells me it's impossible. Most importantly, I know God's plan is bigger and grander than anything I could ever imagine. It just takes some faith to believe it.

How the world treats women impacts how we show up in the world, and vice versa. But what if we begin to recognize our own cracks and brokenness and begin to fix them?

The daily mental noise and struggles rattling in your brain have the ability to make or break us. So why don't you choose the former? Why don't you run headfirst into making amends with your doubts and your fears and change the narrative? It's about time someone told you they're proud of you. It's about time someone told you that you deserve all you strive for and more. It's about time someone said you are enough. Let that someone be you.

Advocate for yourself. Make your mind a good and healthy place to be because the reality is you'll spend a lifetime in your own head. Become your own best friend and follow your gut. You know yourself better than anyone else. While this all sounds cliche and a little cheesy, the simple fact is it's all cliche because it's true.

My biggest hope for those reading this book is that you will slowly but surely learn to break free from the cobwebs you unconsciously got tangled up in so early on in life. My hope is you will learn from both my personal stories and the other women's stories scattered throughout these pages. My hope is you'll use these bits and pieces of information to recognize your own struggles, your own beliefs, and your own mental noise and distractions, and overcome them, bit by bit and day by day.

The road to yourself isn't an easy one, and to be completely honest, I don't think we're ever meant to figure everything out in this life. That's saved for the next. In the meantime, women can push the boundaries, take the risks, and prove others wrong.

Become the entrepreneur you've always wanted to be. Define yourself on your own terms. Strive to heal the parts of yourself that seem too dark to see. Those are always the parts that will show the greatest results.

Most importantly, always remember to choose yourself—because being pretty and young is never all it's cracked up to be.

ACKNOWLEDGMENTS

Writing a book as a first-time author is no easy task—especially in less than a year. It took a village to help me create this work, and I owe a great deal of thanks to everyone who helped me throughout the process, from start to finish. First off, I'd like to thank Eric Koester for creating and leading the Creator Institute—an amazing and seamlessly designed program. Without you, my dreams of being an author would not have come to fruition. Thank you to Amanda Munro, my developmental editor, for brilliantly helping me draft my manuscript from the start. Thank you to Morgana Watson, my marketing and revisions editor, for the weekly pep talks, for your care and attention, and for keeping me on track (even though we know I wasn't the easiest at times). Thank you to the entire team at New Degree Press for helping *Pretty Young* come to life. Thank you to every single woman for graciously allowing me to tell your story; your story is significant. Thank you to every person who pre-ordered my book. Your support meant the world to me. Thank you to my friends for always cheering me on; you all are like sisters to me. Last, but certainly not least, thank you to my parents for teaching me what drive, passion, generosity, and hard work look like. Most importantly, thank you for showing me what unconditional love looks like. God knew it would take a special kind of couple to handle me. Aren't you glad He chose you? I sure am!

APPENDIX

INTRODUCTION

Slaughter, Colleen. "These Stats on Women's Confidence Will Shock You." *Authentic Leadership International (blog),* June 8, 2016. *https://www.boldermoves.com/women-confidence/.*

FACT OR FEELING?

Abrams, Abigail. "Yes, Impostor Syndrome Is Real. Here's How to Deal With It." *Time,* June 20, 2018. *https://time.com/5312483/how-to-deal-with-impostor-syndrome/.*

Adichie, Chimamanda Ngozi. "The Danger of a Single Story." Filmed July 2009. TED video, 4:25. *https://www.ted.com/talks/chimamanda_ngozi_adichie_the_danger_of_a_single_story.*

Bennett, Jessica. "How to Overcome 'Impostor Syndrome.'" *The New York Times,* Accessed on June 5, 2021. *https://www.nytimes.com/guides/working-womans-handbook/overcome-impostor-syndrome.*

Doyle, Glennon. *Untamed.* New York: The Dial Press, 2020.

Gevinson, Tavi. "A Teen Just Trying to Figure It Out." Filmed March 2012. TED video, 4:05. https://www.ted.com/talks/tavi_gevinson_a_teen_just_trying_to_figure_it_out.

Gevinson, Tavi. "A Teen Just Trying to Figure It Out." Filmed March 2012. TED video, 1:10. https://www.ted.com/talks/tavi_gevinson_a_teen_just_trying_to_figure_it_out.

"KPMG Study Finds 75% of Female Executives Across Industries Have Experienced Imposter Syndrome in Their Careers." *KPMG's Women's Leadership*, October 7, 2020. https://womensleadership.kpmg.us/summit/kpmg-womens-leadership-report-2020.html.

McGregor, Jena. "Yet Another Explanation For Why Fewer Women Make it to the Top." *The Washington Post*, November 29, 2011. https://www.washingtonpost.com/blogs/post-leadership/post/yet-another-explanation-for-why-fewer-women-make-it-to-the-top/2011/04/01/gIQA2IIP9N_blog.html?noredirect=on&utm_term=.41cc21a45471.

Nance-Nash, Sheryl. "Why Imposter Syndrome Hits Women and Women of Colour Harder." *BBC*, July 27, 2020. https://www.bbc.com/worklife/article/20200724-why-imposter-syndrome-hits-women-and-women-of-colour-harder.

Young, Valerie. "10 Steps You Can Use to Overcome Imposter Syndrome." *ImposterSyndrome.com*, Accessed June 5, 2021. https://impostorsyndrome.com/10-steps-overcome-impostor/.

CULTURAL PRESSURES

Andrews, Dr. Shawn. "How Culture Impacts Our Value Of Women." *Forbes*, April 6, 2020. https://www.forbes.com/sites/forbescoachescouncil/2020/04/06/how-culture-impacts-our-value-of-women/?sh=1d4abde7474a.

Cherry, Kendra. "Understanding Collectivist Cultures." *VeryWell Mind (blog)*, April 30, 2021. *https://www.verywellmind.com/what-are-collectivistic-cultures-2794962*.

Kaur, Dina, and Verena Daniel. "Column: What It's Like Being Women from Different Cultural Backgrounds." *The State News*, March 10, 2021. *https://statenews.com/article/2021/03/what-its-like-being-women-from-different-cultural-backgrounds*.

YOUR LIMITING BELIEFS ARE LIMITING YOU IN MORE WAYS THAN ONE

Finch, Adrienne, and Sarah Whitney Humphrey. "Making Actionable Goals & Creating Your Roadmap to Success with Adrienne Finch." March 23, 2021. In *It Ain't It, Sis*. Produced by Sarah Whitney. Podcast, MP3 audio, 19.30. *https://podcasts.apple.com/us/podcast/making-actionable-goals-creating-your-roadmap-to-success/id1498493101?i=1000514061430*.

Hoffman Smith, Haley, and Sarah Whitney Humphrey. "Haley Hoffman Smith | Forbes Most Influential Speaker, Author, & Manifestation Coach." September 9, 2020. In *It Ain't It, Sis*. Produced by Sarah Whitney. Podcast, MP3 audio, 22.30. *https://podcasts.apple.com/us/podcast/haley-hoffman-smith-forbes-most-influential-speaker/id1498493101?i=1000490573745*.

Storr, Will. "The Brain's Miracle Superpowers of Self-Improvement." *BBC*, November 24, 2015. *https://www.bbc.com/future/article/20151123-the-brains-miracle-superpowers-of-self-improvement*.

Voss, Patrice, Maryse E. Thomas, J. Miguel Cisneros-Franco, and Étienne de Villers-Sidani. "Dynamic Brains and the Changing Rules of Neuroplasticity: Implications for Learning and Recovery." *Frontiers in Psychology* (2017). *https://doi.org/10.3389/fpsyg.2017.01657*.

REDEFINING BEAUTY ON YOUR OWN TERMS

BuzzFeedVideo. "Women's Ideal Body Types Throughout History." January 26, 2015. Video, 3:09. https://www.youtube.com/watch?v=XrpozJZuoa4.

Pike, MA, LPC, Ellie. "Eating Disorder Statistics—NEDA Week." Eating Recovery Center (blog), February 28, 2020. https://www.eatingrecoverycenter.com/blog/advocacy/Eating-Disorder-Statistics-NEDA-Week-2020.

THE TOXIC TANGO

Bucci, Adriana, and Sarah Whitney Humphrey. "How to Heal from Narcissistic Abuse & Toxic Relationships, & What Doing the 'Inner Work' Actually Looks Like With Adriana Bucci." April 27, 2021. In *It Ain't It, Sis*. Produced by Sarah Whitney. Podcast, MP3 audio, 24.30. https://podcasts.apple.com/us/podcast/how-to-heal-from-narcissistic-abuse-toxic-relationships/id1498493101?i=1000518885918.

#METOO

Kearl, Holly. "Street Harassment of Women: It's a Bigger Problem Than You Think." *The Christian Science Monitor*, April 18, 2011. https://www.csmonitor.com/Commentary/Opinion/2011/0418/Street-harassment-of-women-It-s-a-bigger-problem-than-you-think.

Martin, Gina. "They Told Me to Change My Clothes. I Changed the law Instead." Filmed February 2020. TED video, 5:20. https://www.ted.com/talks/gina_martin_they_told_me_to_change_my_clothes_i_changed_the_law_instead.

RAINN. "Campus Sexual Violence: Statistics." Accessed June 16, 2021. https://www.rainn.org/statistics/campus-sexual-violence.

RAINN. "Scope of the Problem: Statistics." Accessed June 16, 2021. https://www.rainn.org/statistics/scope-problem.

Stop Street Harassment. "About." Accessed June 16, 2021. https://stopstreetharassment.org/about/.

UK Public General Acts, Voyeurism (Offences) Act 2019, https://www.legislation.gov.uk/ukpga/2019/2/section/1/enacted.

US Department of the Interior, National Park Service, Northeast Region, Schoodic: Draft General Management Plan Amendment and Environmental Impact Statement (Maine, 2004), 116, http://purl.fdlp.gov/GPO/gpo67000.

Yale University. "About Yale: Yale Facts." Accessed May 1, 2017. https://www.yale.edu/about-yale/yale-fa

SEXY & I OWN IT

Davis, Stefanie E. "Objectification, Sexualization, and Misrepresentation: Social Media and the College Experience." Social Media + Society, (July 2018). https://doi.org/10.1177/2056305118786727.

Encyclopedia of Sexuality and Gender, "Social Media and Adolescent Sexual Socialization." Accessed June 12, 2021. https://doi.org/10.1007/978-3-319-59531-3_29-1.

Loreck, Janice. "Explainer: What Does the 'Male Gaze' Mean, and What About a Female Gaze." The Conversation, January 5, 2016. https://theconversation.com/explainer-what-does-the-male-gaze-mean-and-what-about-a-female-gaze-52486.

Sheppard, Sarah. "The Sexualization of Young Girls and Mental Health Problems." *VeryWell Mind (blog)*, December 8, 2020. https://www.verywellmind.com/damaging-effects-of-sexualizing-girls-4778062.

FAITH, SHAME & THE PATRIARCHY?

Associated Press. "Roman Catholic dioceses in the US were granted $1.5BILLION in small business relief during the pandemic despite sitting on more than $10billion in cash and assets." *DailyMail.com*, February 4, 2021. https://www.dailymail.co.uk/news/article-9222529/Sitting-billions-Catholic-dioceses-amassed-taxpayer-aid.html.

Brown, Brené. "Listening to Shame." Filmed March 2012. TED video, 18:46. https://www.ted.com/talks/brene_brown_listening_to_shame?language=en#t-1145701.

Dillon, Michele. "The Catholic Church's Euphemization of Power." *National Catholic Reporter*, February 15, 2019. https://www.ncronline.org/news/accountability/catholic-churchs-euphemization-power.

Filipovic, Jill. "America Will Lose More Than Abortion Rights If Roe v. Wade Is Overturned." *Time*, June 28, 2018. https://time.com/5324828/kennedy-retirement-roe-wade-abortion-rights/.

History. "Roe v. Wade." Internet & Research. Updated May 15, 2019. https://www.history.com/topics/womens-rights/roe-v-wade.

King, Jr., Martin Luther. "Loving Your Enemies." Speech presented at the Dexter Avenue Baptist Church in Montgomery, Alabama, December 25, 1957.

Murray, Kelly M., Joseph W. Ciarrocchi, and Nichole A. Murray-Swank. "Spirituality, Religiosity, Shame and Guilt as Predictors of Sexual Attitudes and Experiences." Journal of Psychology and Theology 35, no. 3 (September 2007): 222–34. https://doi.org/10.1177/009164710703500305.

Pew Research Center. "The Divide Over Ordaining Women." Internet & Research. Updated September 9, 2014. https://

www.pewresearch.org/internet/2019/11/15/americans-and-privacy-concerned-confused-and-feeling-lack-of-control-over-their-personal-information/.

Pew Research Center. *Religious Landscape Study.* 2015. https://www.pewforum.org/religious-landscape-study/.

Smith, Judah. "What's the Meaning." January 4, 2021. In *Churchome with Judah Smith.* Produced by Churchome. Podcast, MP3 audio, 22.00. https://podcasts.apple.com/us/podcast/whats-the-meaning/id336817472?i=1000504311157.

Smith, Samuel. "Number of Clergywomen Has Exponentially Increased Over Last 2 Decades, Study Says." *The Christian Post,* October 11, 2018. https://www.christianpost.com/news/number-of-clergywomen-has-exponentially-increased-over-last-2-decades-study-says.html.

THE MENTAL HEALTH PANDEMIC

"Are Young Women More Prone to Mental Health Issues?" *American Addiction Centers: Laguna Treatment Hospital (blog),* February 23, 2021. https://lagunatreatment.com/support-for-women/mental-health-issues/.

Rosenberg, Jamie. "Mental Health Issues On the Rise Among Adolescents, Young Adults." *AJMC (blog),* March 19, 2019. https://www.ajmc.com/view/mental-health-issues-on-the-rise-among-adolescents-young-adults.

Schimelpfening, Nancy. "What Is Dialectical Behavior Therapy (DBT)?" *VeryWell Mind (blog),* May 06, 2021. https://www.verywellmind.com/dialectical-behavior-therapy-1067402.

Sutton, Sadie, and Sarah Whitney Humphrey. "Sadie Sutton | Mental Health Struggles, Treatment, & Persisting Through Tough Times." July 21, 2020. In *It Ain't It, Sis.* Produced by Sarah

Whitney. Podcast, MP3 audio, 12.30. *https://podcasts.apple. com/us/podcast/sadie-sutton-mental-health-struggles-treatment-persisting/id1498493101?i=1000485598188.*

POST-GRAD & A PANDEMIC

Browning, Matthew H. E. M., Lincoln R. Larson, Iryna Sharaievska, Alessandro Rigolon, Olivia McAnirlin, Lauren Mullenbach, Scott Cloutier, Tue M. Vu, Jennifer Thomsen, Nathan Reigner, Elizabeth Covelli Metcalf, Ashley D'Antonio, Marco Helbich, Gregory N. Bratman, and Hector Olvera Alvarez. "Psychological impacts from COVID-19 among university students: Risk factors across seven states in the United States." *PLOS ONE* (Winter 2021). *https://doi.org/10.1371/journal.pone.0245327.*

Desai, Panache. "10 Reasons to Make Inner Peace a Priority." *Gaia (blog)*, May 2, 2019. *https://www.gaia.com/article/10-reasons-make-inner-peace-priority.*

Gilbert, Stephanie. "The Importance of Community and Mental Health." *NAMI (blog)*, November 18, 2019. *https://www.nami.org/Blogs/NAMI-Blog/November-2019/The-Importance-of-Community-and-Mental-Health.*

Prior, Ryan. "1 in 4 Young People are Reporting Suicidal Thoughts. Here's How to Help." *CNN*, August 15, 2020. *https://www.cnn.com/2020/08/14/health/young-people-suicidal-ideation-wellness/index.html.*

ALONE OR LONELY?

Center for Disease Control and Prevention, Morbidity and Mortality Weekly Report (*MMWR*), Mental Health, Substance Use, and Suicidal Ideation During the COVID-19 Pandemic (2020), 1049–1057, *https://www.cdc.gov/mmwr/volumes/69/wr/mm6932a1.htm#suggestedcitation.*

Comer, John Mark. *The Ruthless Elimination of Hurry*. Colorado Springs: WaterBrook, 2019.

"How Social Media Addition Affects Teenagers." *Northwest Primary Care (blog)*, accessed June 18, 2021. https://www.nwpc.com/social-media-addiction-affects-teenagers/.

"Impact of Social Media on Youth Mental Health: Statistics, Tips & Resources." *University of Nevada, Reno (blog)*, Accessed June 18, 2021. https://onlinedegrees.unr.edu/online-master-of-public-health/impact-of-social-media-on-youth-mental-health/.

Miller, Caroline. "Does Social Media Cause Depression?" *Child Mind Institute (blog)*, accessed June 18, 2021. https://childmind.org/article/is-social-media-use-causing-depression/

"Social Media, Social Life: Teens Reveal Their Experiences." Infographic. Common Sense Media, September 10, 2018. https://www.commonsensemedia.org/social-media-social-life-infographic.

Valinsky, Jordan. "Budget Beer and Spiked Seltzer Dominated During the Pandemic." *CNN*, June 10, 2020. https://www.cnn.com/2020/06/09/business/budget-beer-spiked-seltzer-sales-coronavirus/index.html.

VALIDATION IS FOR PARKING

Cascio, Christopher. N., Matthew B. O'Donnell, Francis J. Tinney, Matthew D. Lieberman, Shelley D. Taylor, et al. "Self-Affirmation Activates Brain Systems Associated with Self-Related Processing and Reward and is Reinforced by Future Orientation." *Social Cognitive and Affective Neuroscience*, 11 (2016): 621-629. https://doi.org/10.1093/scan/nsv136.

Dictionary.com. s.v. "validation (*n.*)." Accessed June 19, 2021. http://www.merriam-webster.com/dictionary/app.

Doyle, Glennon. *Untamed*. New York: The Dial Press, 2020.

Hoffman Smith, Haley, and Allyson Byrd. "How to Step Into Your Aligned, Authentic Greatness with Allyson Byrd." December 15, 2020. In *Big Conversations with Haley Hoffman Smith*. Produced by Haley Hoffman Smith. Podcast, MP3 audio, 2.30. https://podcasts.apple.com/us/podcast/how-to-step-into-your-aligned-authentic-greatness-allyson/id1494643478?i=1000502488386.

King, Michael Patrick, dir. Sex and the City. Season 5, episode 6, "Critical Condition." Aired August 25, 2002, on HBO. https://www.hulu.com/watch/229aa466-95c8-4756-8082-33d9f325254b.

McMahan, Janie MA LMFT. "Childhood Emotional Neglect: Why Validation is Vital for Recovery." *Janie McMahan, MA LMFT (blog)*, March 21, 2017. https://www.janiemcmahan.com/blog/2017/3/21/recovering-from-emotional-neglect-why-validation-is-vital.

Saline, Brittney. "4 Ways to Stop Relying on External Validation." *The Talkspace Voice (blog)*, August 5, 2019. https://www.talkspace.com/blog/validation-opinions-stop-seeking/.

WOMEN IN THE WORKPLACE: LACK OF CONFIDENCE & GENDER BIASES

Blakely, Sara. "Finding Your Purpose." Produced by Masterclass. *Masterclass*, 2020. Video, 5:00. https://www.masterclass.com/classes/sara-blakely-teaches-self-made-entrepreneurship/chapters/intro.

Blakely, Sara. "How Spanx Got Started." Produced by INC. Staff. *INC*, January 20, 2012. Video, 1:30. https://www.inc.com/sara-blakely/how-sara-blakley-started-spanx.html.

Boorstin, Julia. "The number of female CEOs is increasing—but here are the big problems standing in their way." *NBC*, January

24, 2020. *https://www.cnbc.com/2020/01/24/number-of-female-ceos-is-increasing-but-they-still-face-glass-cliffs.html.*

Columbia Business School. "Why Aren't Startups Founded by Women Getting More Funding?" Columbia Business School. Press release, April 4, 2019. Columbia Business School. Website. *https://www8.gsb.columbia.edu/newsroom/newsn/6917/why-arent-startups-founded-by-women-getting-more-funding,* accessed June 23, 2021.

Gates, Melinda, and Brené Brown. "Brené with Melinda Gates on The Moment of Lift." January 20, 2021. In *Unlocking Us.* Produced by Parcast. Podcast, MP3 audio, 43:00. *https://brenebrown.com/podcast/brene-with-melinda-gates-on-the-moment-of-lift/#close-popup.*

"Gender Inequality in Film." Infographic. New York Film Academy, 2017. *https://www.nyfa.edu/film-school-blog/gender-inequality-in-film-infographic-updated-in-2018/.*

Include-Empower.com. "Gender Bias at Work: The Assertiveness Double-Bind." Accessed June 25, 2021. *https://culturepluscon-sulting.com/2018/03/10/gender-bias-work-assertiveness-double-bind/.*

Lesonsky, Rieva. "The State of Women Entrepreneurs." Score (blog), March 24, 2020. *https://www.score.org/blog/state-women-en-entrepreneurs.*

Mollick, Ethan. "Why Are There More Male Entrepreneurs Than Female Ones?" December 14, 2015. In *Knowledge@Wharton.* Produced by Wharton, University of Pennsylvania. Podcast, MP3 audio, 4:40. *https://knowledge.wharton.upenn.edu/article/why-are-there-more-male-entrepreneurs-than-female-ones/.*

WOMEN IN THE WORKPLACE: A NEW ERA OF ENTREPRE-ISTAS

Blakely, Sara. "Entrepreneurial Mindset" Produced by Masterclass. *Masterclass*, 2020. Video, 13:20. https://www.masterclass.com/classes/sara-blakely-teaches-self-made-entrepreneurship/chapters/intro.

Philips, Sydney, and Sarah Whitney Humphrey. "Sydney Phillips | Forbes 30 Under 30 Nominee & Boss Babe." June 9, 2020. In *It Ain't It, Sis*. Produced by Sarah Whitney. Podcast, MP3 audio, 15.45. https://podcasts.apple.com/us/podcast/sydney-phillips-forbes-30-under-30-nominee-boss-babe/id1498493101?i=1000477324515.

Williams, Allee, and Sarah Whitney Humphrey. "Allee Williams | Navigating Uncertainty & Trusting the Process." October 6, 2020. In *It Ain't It, Sis*. Produced by Sarah Whitney. Podcast, MP3 audio, 20.30. https://podcasts.apple.com/us/podcast/allee-williams-navigating-uncertainty-trusting-process/id1498493101?i=1000493768251.

www.ingramcontent.com/pod-product-compliance
Lightning Source LLC
LaVergne TN
LVHW011828060526
838200LV00053B/3944